Basic Visual Formatting in CSS

Eric A. Meyer

Beijing · Boston · Farnham · Sebastopol · Tokyo

Basic Visual Formatting in CSS

by Eric A. Meyer

Published by O'Reilly Media, Inc., 1005 Gravenstein Highway North, Sebastopol, CA 95472.

O'Reilly books may be purchased for educational, business, or sales promotional use. Online editions are also available for most titles (*http://safaribooksonline.com*). For more information, contact our corporate/institutional sales department: 800-998-9938 or *corporate@oreilly.com*.

Editor: Meg Foley	**Interior Designer:** David Futato
Production Editor: Colleen Lobner	**Cover Designer:** Ellie Volckhausen
Copyeditor: Amanda Kersey	**Illustrator:** Rebecca Demarest
Proofreader: Lindsy Gamble	

August 2015:   First Edition

Revision History for the First Edition
2015-07-31:   First Release

See *http://oreilly.com/catalog/errata.csp?isbn=9781491929964* for release details.

978-1-491-92996-4

[LSI]

Table of Contents

Preface. v

Basic Visual Formatting. 1
  Basic Boxes   1
    A Quick Refresher   2
    The Containing Block   3
  Altering Element Display   4
    Changing Roles   5
    Block Boxes   7
    Horizontal Formatting   9
    Horizontal Properties   10
    Using auto   11
    More Than One auto   13
    Negative Margins   14
    Percentages   16
    Replaced Elements   17
    Vertical Formatting   18
    Vertical Properties   19
    Percentage Heights   20
    Auto Heights   22
    Collapsing Vertical Margins   23
    Negative Margins and Collapsing   25
    List Items   28
  Inline Elements   28
    Line Layout   29
    Basic Terms and Concepts   32
    Inline Formatting   34
    Inline Nonreplaced Elements   35

Building the Boxes   35
Vertical Alignment   37
Managing the line-height   40
Scaling Line Heights   42
Adding Box Properties   43
Changing Breaking Behavior   46
Glyphs Versus Content Area   47
Inline Replaced Elements   48
Adding Box Properties   49
Replaced Elements and the Baseline   51
Inline-Block Elements   53
Run-in Elements   56
Computed Values   58
Summary   59

Preface

Conventions Used in This Book

The following typographical conventions are used in this book:

Italic
> Indicates new terms, URLs, email addresses, filenames, and file extensions.

`Constant width`
> Used for program listings, as well as within paragraphs to refer to program elements such as variable or function names, databases, data types, environment variables, statements, and keywords.

`Constant width bold`
> Shows commands or other text that should be typed literally by the user.

`Constant width italic`
> Shows text that should be replaced with user-supplied values or by values determined by context.

 This element signifies a general note.

 This element indicates a warning or caution.

Safari® Books Online

 *Safari Books Online* is an on-demand digital library that delivers expert content in both book and video form from the world's leading authors in technology and business.

Technology professionals, software developers, web designers, and business and creative professionals use Safari Books Online as their primary resource for research, problem solving, learning, and certification training.

Safari Books Online offers a range of plans and pricing for enterprise, government, education, and individuals.

Members have access to thousands of books, training videos, and prepublication manuscripts in one fully searchable database from publishers like O'Reilly Media, Prentice Hall Professional, Addison-Wesley Professional, Microsoft Press, Sams, Que, Peachpit Press, Focal Press, Cisco Press, John Wiley & Sons, Syngress, Morgan Kaufmann, IBM Redbooks, Packt, Adobe Press, FT Press, Apress, Manning, New Riders, McGraw-Hill, Jones & Bartlett, Course Technology, and hundreds more. For more information about Safari Books Online, please visit us online.

How to Contact Us

Please address comments and questions concerning this book to the publisher:

O'Reilly Media, Inc.
1005 Gravenstein Highway North
Sebastopol, CA 95472
800-998-9938 (in the United States or Canada)
707-829-0515 (international or local)
707-829-0104 (fax)

We have a web page for this book, where we list errata, examples, and any additional information. You can access this page at *http://bit.ly/basic-visual-formatting*.

To comment or ask technical questions about this book, send email to *bookquestions@oreilly.com*.

For more information about our books, courses, conferences, and news, see our website at *http://www.oreilly.com*.

Find us on Facebook: *http://facebook.com/oreilly*

Follow us on Twitter: *http://twitter.com/oreillymedia*

Watch us on YouTube: *http://www.youtube.com/oreillymedia*

Basic Visual Formatting

This book is all about the theoretical side of visual rendering in CSS. Why is it necessary to spend an entire book (however slim) on the theoretical underpinnings of visual rendering? The answer is that with a model as open and powerful as that contained within CSS, no book could hope to cover every possible way of combining properties and effects. You will obviously go on to discover new ways of using CSS. In the course of exploring CSS, you may encounter seemingly strange behaviors in user agents. With a thorough grasp of how the visual rendering model works in CSS, you'll be able to determine whether a behavior is a correct (if unexpected) consequence of the rendering engine CSS defines, or whether you've stumbled across a bug that needs to be reported.

Basic Boxes

At its core, CSS assumes that every element generates one or more rectangular boxes, called *element boxes*. (Future versions of the specification may allow for nonrectangular boxes, and indeed there are proposals to change this, but for now everything is rectangular.) Each element box has a *content area* at its center. This content area is surrounded by optional amounts of padding, borders, outlines, and margins. These areas are considered optional because they could all be set to a width of zero, effectively removing them from the element box. An example content area is shown in Figure 1, along with the surrounding regions of padding, borders, and margins.

Each of the margins, borders, and the padding can be set using various side-specific properties, such as `margin-left` or `border-bottom`, as well as shorthand properties such as `padding`. The outline, if any, does not have side-specific properties. The content's background—a color or tiled image, for example—is applied within the padding by default. The margins are always transparent, allowing the background(s) of any parent element(s) to be visible. Padding cannot have a negative length, but margins can. We'll explore the effects of negative margins later on.

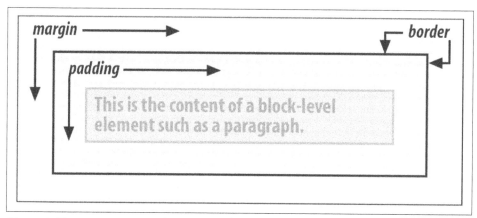

Figure 1. The content area and its surroundings

Borders are generated using defined styles, such as `solid` or `inset`, and their colors are set using the `border-color` property. If no color is set, then the border takes on the foreground color of the element's content. For example, if the text of a paragraph is white, then any borders around that paragraph will be white, *unless* the author explicitly declares a different border color. If a border style has gaps of some type, then the element's background is visible through those gaps by default. Finally, the width of a border can never be negative.

The various components of an element box can be affected via a number of properties, such as `width` or `border-right`. Many of these properties will be used in this book, even though they aren't defined here.

A Quick Refresher

Let's quickly review the kinds of boxes we'll be discussing, as well as some important terms that are needed to follow the explanations to come:

Normal flow
> This is the left-to-right, top-to-bottom rendering of text in Western languages and the familiar text layout of traditional HTML documents. Note that the flow direction may be changed in non-Western languages. Most elements are in the normal flow, and the only way for an element to leave the normal flow is to be floated, positioned, or made into a flexible box or grid layout element. Remember, the discussions in this chapter cover only elements in the normal flow.

Nonreplaced element
> This is an element whose content is contained within the document. For example, a paragraph (p) is a nonreplaced element because its textual content is found within the element itself.

Replaced element

This is an element that serves as a placeholder for something else. The classic example of a replaced element is the `img` element, which simply points to an image file that is inserted into the document's flow at the point where the `img` element itself is found. Most form elements are also replaced (e.g., `<input type="radio">`).

Root element

This is the element at the top of the document tree. In HTML documents, this is the element `html`. In XML documents, it can be whatever the language permits; for example, the root element of RSS files is `rss`.

Block box

This is a box that an element such as a paragraph, heading, or `div` generates. These boxes generate "new lines" both before and after their boxes when in the normal flow so that block boxes in the normal flow stack vertically, one after another. Any element can be made to generate a block box by declaring `display: block`.

Inline box

This is a box that an element such as `strong` or `span` generates. These boxes do not generate "linebreaks" before or after themselves. Any element can be made to generate an inline box by declaring `display: inline`.

Inline-block box

This is a box that is like a block box internally, but acts like an inline box externally. It acts similar to, but not quite the same as, a replaced element. Imagine picking up a `div` and sticking it into a line of text as if it were an inline image, and you've got the idea.

There are several other types of boxes, such as table-cell boxes, but they won't be covered in this book for a variety of reasons—not the least of which is that their complexity demands a book of its own, and very few authors will actually wrestle with them on a regular basis.

The Containing Block

There is one more kind of box that we need to examine in detail, and in this case enough detail that it merits its own section: the *containing block*.

Every element's box is laid out with respect to its containing block; in a very real way, the containing block is the "layout context" for a box. CSS defines a series of rules for determining a box's containing block. We'll cover only those rules that pertain to the concepts covered in this book in order to keep our focus.

For an element in the normal, Western-style flow of text, the containing block forms from the *content edge* of the nearest ancestor that generated a list item or block box, which includes all table-related boxes (e.g., those generated by table cells). Consider the following markup:

```
<body>
    <div>
        <p>This is a paragraph.</p>
    </div>
</body>
```

In this very simple markup, the containing block for the p element's block box is the div element's block box, as that is the closest ancestor element box that is a block or a list item (in this case, it's a block box). Similarly, the div's containing block is the body's box. Thus, the layout of the p is dependent on the layout of the div, which is in turn dependent on the layout of the body element.

And above that, the layout of the body element is dependent on the layout of the html element, whose box creates what is called the *initial containing block*. It's a little bit unique in that the viewport—the browser window in screen media, or the printable area of the page in print media—determines its dimensions, not the size of the content of the root element. It's a subtle distinction, and usually not a very important one, but it does exist.

Altering Element Display

You can affect the way a user agent displays by setting a value for the property display. Now that we've taken a close look at visual formatting, let's consider the display property and discuss two more of its values using concepts from earlier in the book.

---

display

Values:	none | inline | block | inline-block | list-item | run-in | table | inline-table | table-row-group | table-header-group | table-footer-group | table-row | table-column-group | table-column | table-cell | table-caption | inherit
Initial value:	inline
Applies to:	All elements
Inherited:	No

Computed value:	Varies for floated, positioned, and root elements (see CSS2.1, section 9.7); otherwise, as specified

We'll ignore the table-related values, since they're far too complex for this text, and we'll also ignore the value list-item since it's very similar to block boxes. We've spent quite some time discussing block and inline boxes, but let's spend a moment talking about how altering an element's display role can alter layout before we look at inline-block and run-in.

Changing Roles

When it comes to styling a document, it's obviously handy to be able to change the type of box an element generates. For example, suppose we have a series of links in a nav that we'd like to lay out as a vertical sidebar:

```
<nav>
    <a href="index.html">WidgetCo Home</a>
    <a href="products.html">Products</a>
    <a href="services.html">Services</a>
    <a href="fun.html">Widgety Fun!</a>
    <a href="support.html">Support</a>
    <a href="about.html" id="current">About Us</a>
    <a href="contact.html">Contact</a>
</nav>
```

We could put all the links into table cells, or wrap each one in its own nav—or we could just make them all block-level elements, like this:

```
nav a {display: block;}
```

This will make every a element within the navigation nav a block-level element. If we add on a few more styles, we could have a result like that shown in Figure 2.

Figure 2. Changing the display role from inline to block

Changing display roles can be useful in cases where you want non-CSS browsers to get the navigation links as inline elements but to lay out the same links as block-level elements. With the links as blocks, you can style them as you would div or p elements, with the advantage that the entire element box becomes part of the link. Thus, if a user's mouse pointer hovers anywhere in the element box, she can then click the link.

You may also want to take elements and make them inline. Suppose we have an unordered list of names:

```
<ul id="rollcall">
    <li>Bob C.</li>
    <li>Marcio G.</li>
    <li>Eric M.</li>
    <li>Kat M.</li>
    <li>Tristan N.</li>
    <li>Arun R.</li>
    <li>Doron R.</li>
    <li>Susie W.</li>
</ul>
```

Given this markup, say we want to make the names into a series of inline names with vertical bars between them (and on each end of the list). The only way to do so is to change their display role. The following rules will have the effect shown in Figure 3:

```
#rollcall li {display: inline; border-right: 1px solid; padding: 0 0.33em;}
#rollcall li:first-child {border-left: 1px solid;}
```

| Bob C. | Marcio G. | Eric M. | Kat M. | Tristan N. | Arun R. | Doron R. | Susie W. |

Figure 3. Changing the display role from list-item to inline

There are plenty of other ways to use display to your advantage in design. Be creative and see what you can invent!

Be careful to note, however, that you are changing the display role of elements—not changing their inherent nature. In other words, causing a paragraph to generate an inline box does *not* turn that paragraph into an inline element. In XHTML, for example, some elements are block while others are inline. (Still others are "flow" elements, but we're ignoring them right now.) An inline element can be a descendant of a block element, but the reverse is not true. Thus, while a span can be placed inside a paragraph, a span cannot be wrapped around a paragraph. This will hold true no matter how you style the elements in question. Consider the following markup:

```
<span style="display: block;">
<p style="display: inline;">this is wrong!</p>
</span>
```

The markup will not validate because the block element (p) is nested inside an inline element (span). The changing of display roles does nothing to change this. display has its name because it affects how the element is displayed, not because it changes what kind of element it is.

With that said, let's get into the details of different kinds of boxes: block boxes, inline boxes, inline-block boxes, list-item boxes, and run-in boxes.

Block Boxes

Block boxes can behave in sometimes predictable, sometimes surprising ways. The handling of box placement along the horizontal and vertical axes can differ, for example. In order to fully understand how block boxes are handled, you must clearly understand a number of boundaries and areas. They are shown in detail in Figure 4.

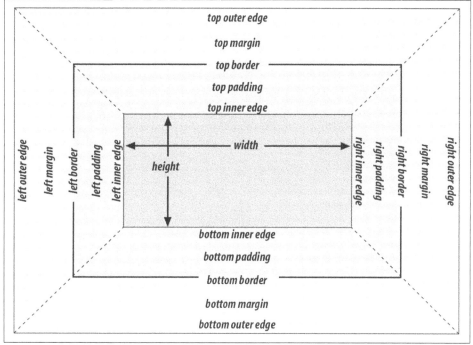

Figure 4. The complete box model

By default, the width of a block box is defined to be the distance from the left inner edge to the right inner edge, and the height is the distance from the inner top to the inner bottom. Both of these properties can be applied to an element generating a block box. It's also the case that we can alter how these properties are treated using the property box-sizing.

box-sizing

Values:	content-box | padding-box | border-box | inherit
Initial value:	content-box
Applies to:	All elements that accept width or height values
Inherited:	No
Computed value:	As specified

This property is how you change what the width and height values actually do. If you declare width: 400px and don't declare a value for box-sizing, then the element's content box will be 400 pixels wide; any padding, borders, and so on will be added to it. If, on the other hand, you declare box-sizing: border-box, then it will be 400 pixels from the left outer border edge to the right outer border edge; any border or padding will be placed within that distance, thus shrinking the width of the content area. This is illustrated in Figure 5.

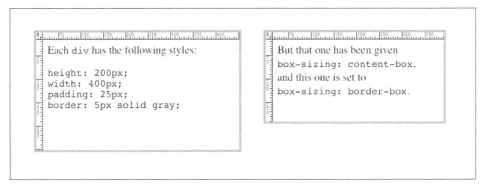

Figure 5. The effects of box-sizing

We're talking about the box-sizing property here because, as stated, it applies to "all elements that accept width or height values." That's most often elements generating block boxes, though it also applies to replaced inline elements like images as well as inline-block boxes.

The various widths, heights, padding, and margins all combine to determine how a document is laid out. In most cases, the height and width of the document are automatically determined by the browser and are based on the available display region, plus other factors. With CSS, of course, you can assert more direct control over the way elements are sized and displayed.

Horizontal Formatting

Horizontal formatting is often more complex than you'd think. Part of the complexity has to do with the default behavior of box-sizing. With the default value of content-box, the value given for width affects the width of the content area, *not* the entire visible element box. Consider the following example:

```
<p style="width: 200px;">wideness?</p>
```

This will make the paragraph's content 200 pixels wide. If we give the element a background, this will be quite obvious. However, any padding, borders, or margins you specify are *added* to the width value. Suppose we do this:

```
<p style="width: 200px; padding: 10px; margin: 20px;">wideness?</p>
```

The visible element box is now 220 pixels wide, since we've added 10 pixels of padding to the right and left of the content. The margins will now extend another 20 pixels to both sides for an overall element box width of 260 pixels. This is illustrated in Figure 6.

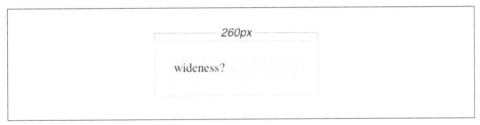

Figure 6. Additive padding and margin

Of course, if we change the styles to use the border box for box-sizing, then the results would be different. In that case, the visible box would be 200 pixels wide with a content width of 180 pixels, and a total of 40 pixels of margin to the sides, giving an overall box width of 240 pixels, as illustrated in Figure 7.

In either case, there is a simple rule that says that the sum of the horizontal components of a block box in the normal flow always equals the width of the containing block. Let's consider two paragraphs within a div whose margins have been set to be 1em, and whose box-sizing value is the default. The content width (the value of width) of each paragraph, plus its left and right padding, borders, and margins, always adds up to the width of the div's content area.

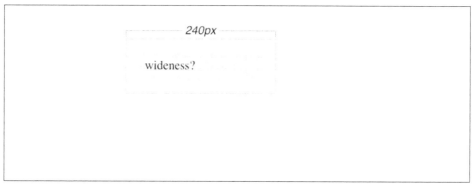

Figure 7. Subtracted padding

Let's say the width of the div is 30em. That makes the sum total of the content width, padding, borders, and margins of each paragraph 30 em. In Figure 8, the "blank" space around the paragraphs is actually their margins. If the div had any padding, there would be even more blank space, but that isn't the case here.

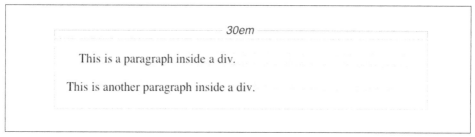

Figure 8. Element boxes are as wide as the width of their containing block

Horizontal Properties

The "seven properties" of horizontal formatting are: margin-left, border-left, padding-left, width, padding-right, border-right, and margin-right. These properties relate to the horizontal layout of block boxes and are diagrammed in Figure 9.

The values of these seven properties must add up to the width of the element's containing block, which is usually the value of width for a block element's parent (since block-level elements nearly always have block-level elements for parents).

Of these seven properties, only three may be set to auto: the width of the element's content and the left and right margins. The remaining properties must be set either to specific values or default to a width of zero. Figure 10 shows which parts of the box can take a value of auto and which cannot.

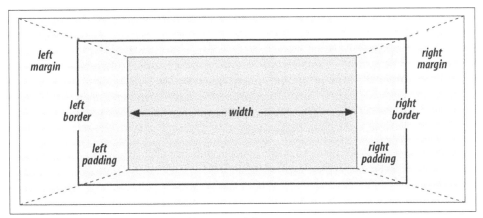

Figure 9. The "seven properties" of horizontal formatting

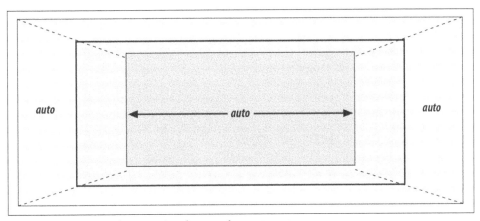

Figure 10. Horizontal properties that can be set to auto

width must either be set to auto or a nonnegative value of some type. When you do use auto in horizontal formatting, different effects can occur.

Using auto

If you set width, margin-left, or margin-right to a value of auto, and give the remaining two properties specific values, then the property that is set to auto is set to the length required to make the element box's width equal to the parent element's width. In other words, let's say the sum of the seven properties must equal 500 pixels, no padding or borders are set, the right margin and width are set to 100px, and the left margin is set to auto. The left margin will thus be 300 pixels wide:

```
div {width: 500px;}
p {margin-left: auto; margin-right: 100px;
    width: 100px;} /* 'auto' left margin evaluates to 300px */
```

In a sense, `auto` can be used to make up the difference between everything else and the required total. However, what if all three of these properties are set to `100px` and *none* of them are set to `auto`?

In the case where all three properties are set to something other than `auto`—or, in CSS terminology, when these formatting properties have been *overconstrained*—then `margin-right` is *always* forced to be `auto`. This means that if both margins and the width are set to `100px`, then the user agent will reset the right margin to `auto`. The right margin's width will then be set according to the rule that one `auto` value "fills in" the distance needed to make the element's overall width equal that of its containing block. Figure 11 shows the result of the following markup:

```
div {width: 500px;}
p {margin-left: 100px; margin-right: 100px;
    width: 100px;} /* right margin forced to be 300px */
```

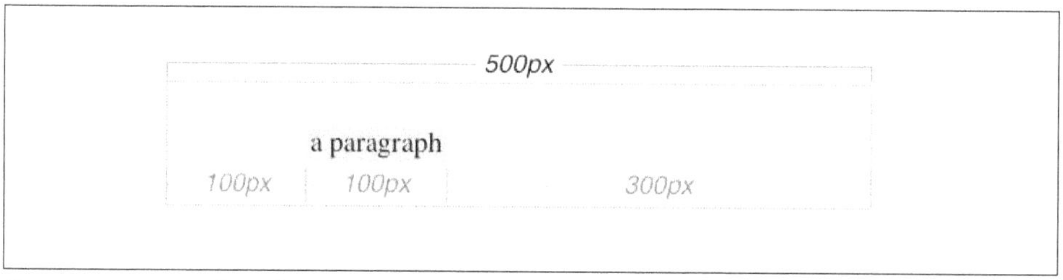

Figure 11. Overriding the margin-right setting

If both margins are set explicitly, and `width` is set to `auto`, then `width` will be whatever value is needed to reach the required total (which is the content width of the parent element). The results of the following markup are shown in Figure 12:

```
p {margin-left: 100px; margin-right: 100px; width: auto;}
```

The case shown in Figure 12 is the most common case, since it is equivalent to setting the margins and not declaring anything for the `width`. The result of the following markup is exactly the same as that shown in Figure 12:

```
p {margin-left: 100px; margin-right: 100px;} /* same as before */
```

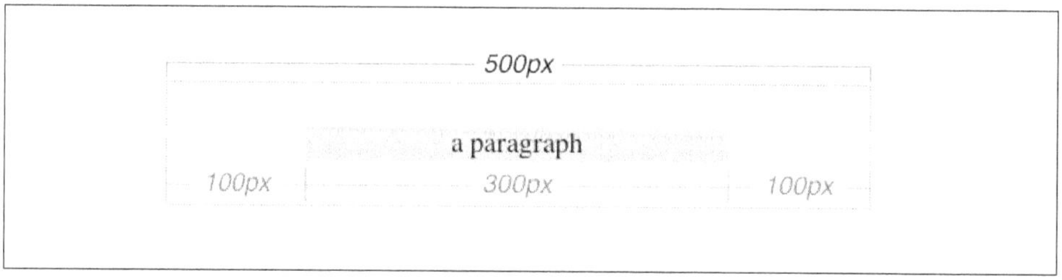

Figure 12. Automatic width

You might be wondering what happens if `box-sizing` is set to, say, `padding-box`. The discussion here tends to assume that the default of `content-box` is used, but all the same principles described here apply, which is why this section only talked about `width` and the side margins without introducing any padding or borders. The handling of `width: auto` in this section and the following sections is the same regardless of the value of `box-sizing`. The details of what gets placed where inside the box-sizing-defined box may vary, but the treatment of `auto` values does not, because `box-sizing` determines what `width` refers to, not how it behaves in relation to the margins.

More Than One auto

Now let's see what happens when two of the three properties (`width`, `margin-left`, and `margin-right`) are set to `auto`. If both margins are set to `auto`, as shown in the following code, then they are set to equal lengths, thus centering the element within its parent. This is illustrated in Figure 13.

```
div {width: 500px;}
p {width: 300px; margin-left: auto; margin-right: auto;}
    /* each margin is 100 pixels wide, because (500-300)/2 = 100 */
```

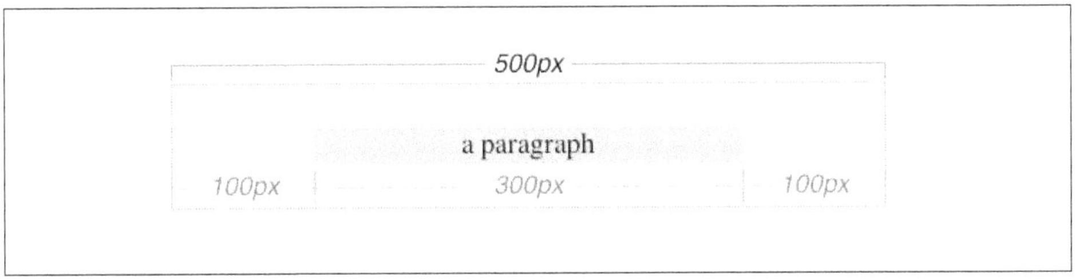

Figure 13. Setting an explicit width

Setting both margins to equal lengths is the correct way to center elements within block boxes in the normal flow. (There are other methods to be found with flexible box and grid layout, but they're beyond the scope of this text.)

Another way of sizing elements is to set one of the margins and the `width` to `auto`. The margin set to be `auto` is reduced to zero:

```
div {width: 500px;}
p {margin-left: auto; margin-right: 100px;
    width: auto;} /* left margin evaluates to 0; width becomes 400px */
```

The `width` is then set to the value necessary to make the element fill its containing block; in the preceding example, it would be 400 pixels, as shown in Figure 14.

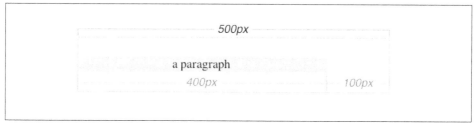

Figure 14. What happens when both the width and right margin are auto

Finally, what happens when all three properties are set to auto? The answer is simple: both margins are set to zero, and the width is made as wide as possible. This result is the same as the default situation, when no values are explicitly declared for margins or the width. In such a case, the margins default to zero and the width defaults to auto.

Note that since horizontal margins do not collapse, the padding, borders, and margins of a parent element can affect its children. The effect is indirect in that the margins (and so on) of an element can induce an offset for child elements. The results of the following markup are shown in Figure 15:

```
div {padding: 50px; background: silver;}
p {margin: 30px; padding: 0; background: white;}
```

Negative Margins

So far, this probably all seems rather straightforward, and you may be wondering why I said things could be complicated. Well, there's another side to margins: the negative side. That's right, it's possible to set negative values for margins. Setting negative margins can result in some interesting effects.

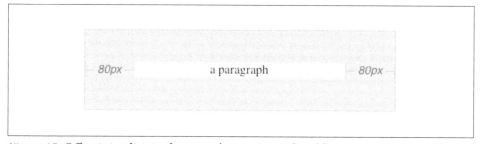

Figure 15. Offset is implicit in the parent's margins and padding

Remember that the total of the seven horizontal properties always equals the width of the parent element. As long as all properties are zero or greater, an element can never be wider than its parent's content area. However, consider the following markup, depicted in Figure 16:

```
div {width: 500px; border: 3px solid black;}
p.wide {margin-left: 10px; width: auto; margin-right: -50px; }
```

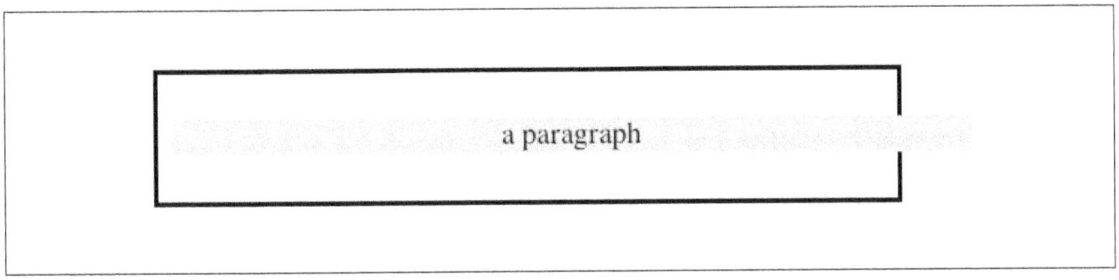

Figure 16. Wider children through negative margins

Yes indeed, the child element is wider than its parent! This is mathematically correct:

```
10px + 0 + 0 + 540px + 0 + 0 - 50px = 500px
```

The 540px is the evaluation of width: auto, which is the number needed to balance out the rest of the values in the equation. Even though it leads to a child element sticking out of its parent, the specification hasn't been violated because the values of the seven properties add up to the required total. It's a semantic dodge, but it's valid behavior.

Now, let's add some borders to the mix:

```
div {width: 500px; border: 3px solid black;}
p.wide {margin-left: 10px; width: auto; margin-right: -50px;
    border: 3px solid gray;}
```

The resulting change will be a reduction in the evaluated width of width:

```
10px + 3px + 0 + 534px + 0 + 3px - 50px = 500px
```

If we were to introduce padding, then the value of width would drop even more.

Conversely, it's possible to have auto right margins evaluate to negative amounts. If the values of other properties force the right margin to be negative in order to satisfy the requirement that elements be no wider than their containing block, then that's what will happen. Consider:

```
div {width: 500px; border: 3px solid black;}
p.wide {margin-left: 10px; width: 600px; margin-right: auto;
    border: 3px solid gray;}
```

The equation will work out like this:

```
10px + 3px + 0 + 600px + 0 + 3px - 116px = 500px
```

The right margin will evaluate to -116px. Even if we'd given it a different explicit value, it would still be forced to -116px because of the rule stating that when an element's dimensions are overconstrained, the right margin is reset to whatever is needed to make the numbers work out correctly. (Except in right-to-left languages, where the left margin would be overruled instead.)

Let's consider another example, illustrated in Figure 17, where the left margin is set to be negative:

```
div {width: 500px; border: 3px solid black;}
p.wide {margin-left: -50px; width: auto; margin-right: 10px;
    border: 3px solid gray;}
```

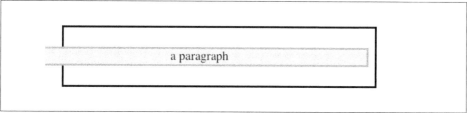

Figure 17. Setting a negative left margin

With a negative left margin, not only does the paragraph spill beyond the borders of the div, but it also spills beyond the edge of the browser window itself!

Remember that padding, borders, and content widths (and heights) can never be negative. Only margins can be less than zero.

Percentages

When it comes to percentage values for the width, padding, and margins, the same basic rules apply. It doesn't really matter whether the values are declared with lengths or percentages.

Percentages can be very useful. Suppose we want an element's content to be two-thirds the width of its containing block, the right and left padding to be 5% each, the left margin to be 5%, and the right margin to take up the slack. That would be written something like:

```
<p style="width: 67%; padding-right: 5%; padding-left: 5%; margin-right: auto;
    margin-left: 5%;">playing percentages</p>
```

The right margin would evaluate to 18% (100% - 67% - 5% - 5% - 5%) of the width of the containing block.

Mixing percentages and length units can be tricky, however. Consider the following example:

```
<p style="width: 67%; padding-right: 2em; padding-left: 2em; margin-right: auto;
    margin-left: 5em;">mixed lengths</p>
```

In this case, the element's box can be defined like this:

```
5em + 0 + 2em + 67% + 2em + 0 + auto = containing block width
```

In order for the right margin's width to evaluate to zero, the element's containing block must be 27.272727 em wide (with the content area of the element being 18.272727 em wide). Any wider than that, and the right margin will evaluate to a positive value. Any narrower and the right margin will be a negative value.

The situation gets even more complicated if we start mixing length-value unity types, like this:

```
<p style="width: 67%; padding-right: 15px; padding-left: 10px;
    margin-right: auto;
    margin-left: 5em;">more mixed lengths</p>
```

And, just to make things more complex, borders cannot accept percentage values, only length values. The bottom line is that it isn't really possible to create a fully flexible element based solely on percentages unless you're willing to avoid using borders or use some of the more experimental approaches such as flexible box layout.

Replaced Elements

So far, we've been dealing with the horizontal formatting of nonreplaced block boxes in the normal flow of text. Block-level replaced elements are a bit simpler to manage. All of the rules given for nonreplaced blocks hold true, with one exception: if width is auto, then the width of the element is the content's intrinsic width. The image in the following example will be 20 pixels wide because that's the width of the original image:

```
<img src="smile.svg" style="display: block; width: auto; margin: 0;">
```

If the actual image were 100 pixels wide instead, then it would be laid out as 100 pixels wide.

It's possible to override this rule by assigning a specific value to width. Suppose we modify the previous example to show the same image three times, each with a different width value:

```
<img src="smile.svg" style="display: block; width: 25px; margin: 0;">
<img src="smile.svg" style="display: block; width: 50px; margin: 0;">
<img src="smile.svg" style="display: block; width: 100px; margin: 0;">
```

This is illustrated in Figure 18.

Note that the height of the elements also increases. When a replaced element's width is changed from its intrinsic width, the value of height is scaled to match, unless height has been set to an explicit value of its own. The reverse is also true: if height is set, but width is left as auto, then the width is scaled proportionately to the change in height.

Figure 18. Changing replaced element widths

Now that you're thinking about height, let's move on to the vertical formatting of normal-flow block box.

Vertical Formatting

Like horizontal formatting, the vertical formatting of block boxes has its own set of interesting behaviors. An element's content determines the default height of an element. The width of the content also affects height; the skinnier a paragraph becomes, for example, the taller it has to be in order to contain all of the inline content within it.

In CSS, it is possible to set an explicit height on any block-level element. If you do this, the resulting behavior depends on several other factors. Assume that the specified height is greater than that needed to display the content:

```
<p style="height: 10em;">
```

In this case, the extra height has a visual effect somewhat like extra padding. But suppose the height is *less* than what is needed to display the content:

```
<p style="height: 3.33em;">
```

When that happens, the browser is supposed to provide a means of viewing all content without increasing the height of the element box. In a case where the content of an element is taller than the height of its box, the actual behavior of a user agent will depend on the value of the property `overflow`. Two alternatives are shown in Figure 19.

Under CSS1, user agents can ignore any value of `height` other than `auto` if an element is not a replaced element (such as an image). In CSS2 and later, the value of `height` cannot be ignored, except in one specific circumstance involving percentage values. We'll talk about that in a moment.

Just as with `width`, `height` defines the content area's height by default, as opposed to the height of the visible element box. Any padding, borders, or margins on the top or bottom of the element box are *added* to the value for height, unless the value of `box-sizing` is different than `content-box`.

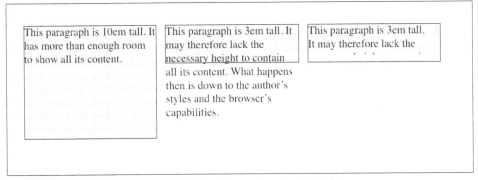

Figure 19. Heights that don't match the element's content height

Vertical Properties

As was the case with horizontal formatting, vertical formatting also has seven related properties: `margin-top`, `border-top`, `padding-top`, `height`, `padding-bottom`, `border-bottom`, and `margin-bottom`. These properties are diagrammed in Figure 20.

The values of these seven properties must equal the height of the block box's containing block. This is usually the value of `height` for a block box's parent (since block-level elements nearly always have block-level elements for parents).

Only three of these seven properties may be set to `auto`: the `height` of the element, and the top and bottom margins. The top and bottom padding and borders must be set to specific values or else they default to a width of zero (assuming no border-style is declared). If `border-style` has been set, then the thickness of the borders is set to be the vaguely defined value `medium`. Figure 21 provides an illustration for remembering which parts of the box may have a value of `auto` and which may not.

Interestingly, if either `margin-top` or `margin-bottom` is set to `auto` for a block box in the normal flow, they both automatically evaluate to `0`. A value of `0` unfortunately prevents easy vertical centering of normal-flow boxes in their containing blocks. It also means that if you set the top and bottom margins of an element to `auto`, they are effectively reset to `0` and removed from the element box.

The handling of `auto` top and bottom margins is different for positioned elements, as well as flexible-box elements.

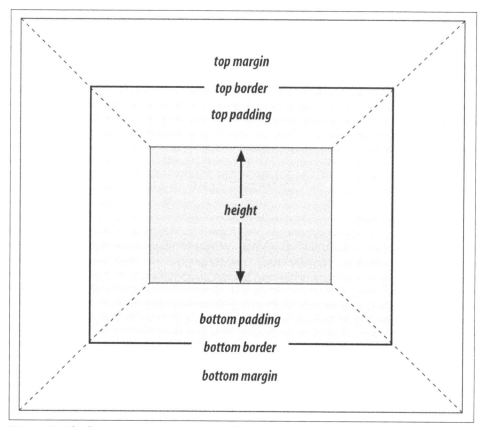

Figure 20. The "seven properties" of vertical formatting

`height` must be set to `auto` or to a nonnegative value of some type; it can never be less than zero.

Percentage Heights

You already saw how length-value heights are handled, so let's spend a moment on percentages. If the height of a normal-flow block box is set to a percentage value, then that value is taken as a percentage of the height of the box's containing block. Given the following markup, the resulting paragraph will be 3 em tall:

```
<div style="height: 6em;">
    <p style="height: 50%;">Half as tall</p>
</div>
```

Since setting the top and bottom margins to `auto` will give them zero height, the only way to vertically center the element in this particular case would be to set them both to 25%—and even then, the box would be centered, not the content within it.

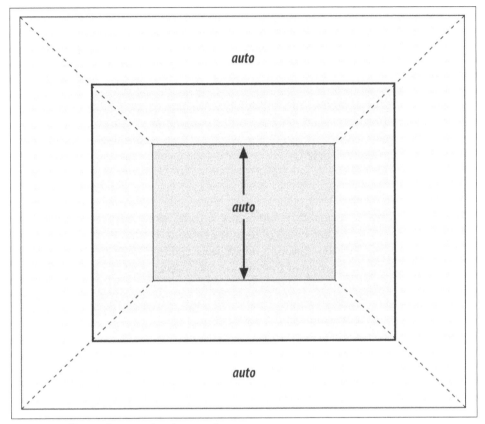

Figure 21. Vertical properties that can be set to auto

However, in cases where the height of the containing block is *not* explicitly declared, percentage heights are reset to `auto`. If we changed the previous example so that the `height` of the `div` is `auto`, the paragraph will now be exactly as tall as the `div` itself:

```
<div style="height: auto;">
    <p style="height: 50%;">NOT half as tall; height reset to auto</p>
</div>
```

These two possibilities are illustrated in Figure 22. (The spaces between the paragraph borders and the `div` borders are the top and bottom margins on the paragraphs.)

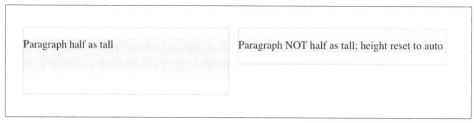

Figure 22. Percentage heights in different circumstances

Before we move on, take a closer look at the first example in Figure 22, the half-as-tall paragraph. It may be half as tall, but it isn't vertically centered. That's because the containing div is 6 em tall, which means the half-as-tall paragraph is 3 em tall. It has top and bottom margins of 1 em, so its overall box height is 5 em. That means there is actually 2 em of space between the bottom of the paragraph's visible box and the div's bottom border, not 1 em. It might seem a bit odd at first glance, but it makes sense once you work through the details.

Auto Heights

In the simplest case, a normal-flow block box with height: auto is rendered just high enough to enclose the line boxes of its inline content (including text). If an auto-height, normal-flow block box has only block-level children, then its default height will be the distance from the top of the topmost block-level child's outer border edge to the bottom of the bottommost block-level child's outer bottom border edge. Therefore, the margins of the child elements will "stick out" of the element that contains them. (This behavior is explained in the next section.)

However, if the block-level element has either top or bottom padding, or top or bottom borders, then its height will be the distance from the top of the outer-top margin edge of its topmost child to the outer-bottom margin edge of its bottommost child:

```
<div style="height: auto;
    background: silver;">
    <p style="margin-top: 2em; margin-bottom: 2em;">A paragraph!</p>
</div>
<div style="height: auto; border-top: 1px solid; border-bottom: 1px solid;
    background: silver;">
    <p style="margin-top: 2em; margin-bottom: 2em;">Another paragraph!</p>
</div>
```

Both of these behaviors are demonstrated in Figure 23.

If we changed the borders in the previous example to padding, the effect on the height of the div would be the same: it would still enclose the paragraph's margins within it.

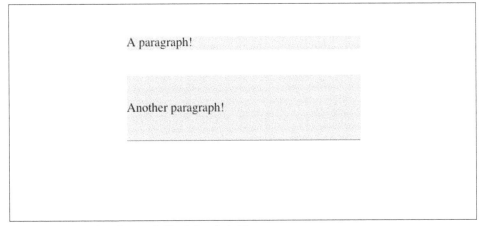

Figure 23. Auto heights with block-level children

Collapsing Vertical Margins

One other important aspect of vertical formatting is the *collapsing* of vertically adjacent margins. Collapsing behavior applies only to margins. Padding and borders, where they exist, never collapse with anything.

An unordered list, where list items follow one another, is a perfect example of margin collapsing. Assume that the following is declared for a list that contains five items:

```
li {margin-top: 10px; margin-bottom: 15px;}
```

Each list item has a 10-pixel top margin and a 15-pixel bottom margin. When the list is rendered, however, the distance between adjacent list items is 15 pixels, not 25. This happens because, along the vertical axis, adjacent margins are collapsed. In other words, the smaller of the two margins is eliminated in favor of the larger. Figure 24 shows the difference between collapsed and uncollapsed margins.

Correctly implemented user agents collapse vertically adjacent margins, as shown in the first list in Figure 24, where there are 15-pixel spaces between each list item. The second list shows what would happen if the user agent didn't collapse margins, resulting in 25-pixel spaces between list items.

Another word to use, if you don't like "collapse," is "overlap." Although the margins are not really overlapping, you can visualize what's happening using the following analogy.

Imagine that each element, such as a paragraph, is a small piece of paper with the content of the element written on it. Around each piece of paper is some amount of clear plastic, which represents the margins. The first piece of paper (say an h1 piece) is laid down on the canvas. The second (a paragraph) is laid below it and then slid up until the edge of one of the piece's plastic touches the edge of the other's paper. If the first piece of paper has half an inch of plastic along its bottom edge, and the second has a third of an inch along its top, then when they slide together, the first piece's plastic will touch the top edge of the second piece of paper. The two are now done being placed on the canvas, and the plastic attached to the pieces is overlapping.

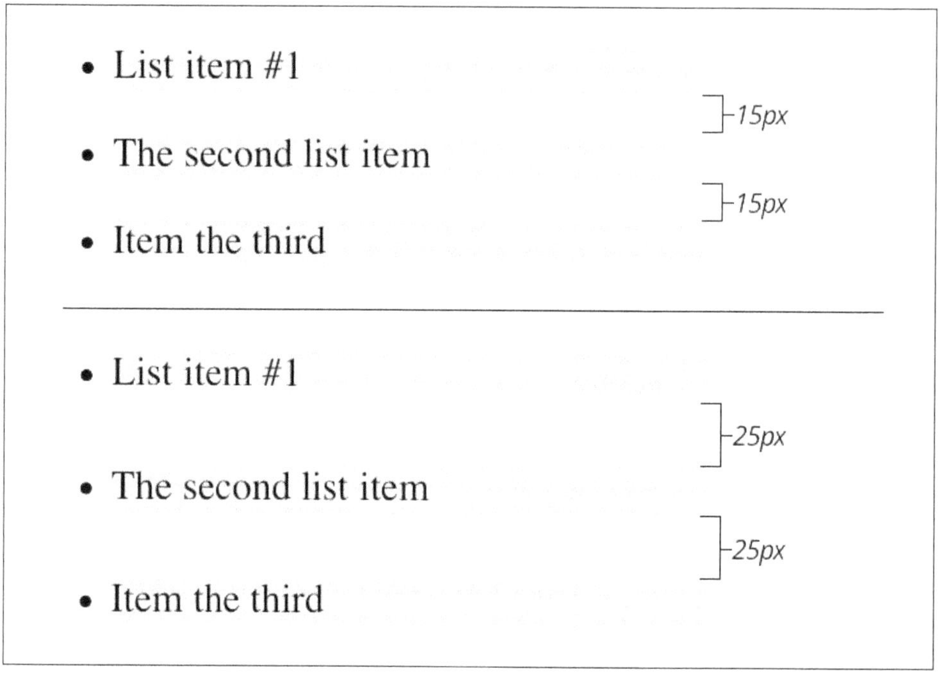

Figure 24. Collapsed versus uncollapsed margins

Collapsing also occurs where multiple margins meet, such as at the end of a list. Adding to the earlier example, let's assume the following rules apply:

```
ul {margin-bottom: 15px;}
li {margin-top: 10px; margin-bottom: 20px;}
h1 {margin-top: 28px;}
```

The last item in the list has a bottom margin of 20 pixels, the bottom margin of the ul is 15 pixels, and the top margin of a succeeding h1 is 28 pixels. So once the margins have been collapsed, the distance between the end of the li and the beginning of the h1 is 28 pixels, as shown in Figure 25.

Now, recall the examples from the previous section, where the introduction of a border or padding on a containing block would cause the margins of its child elements to be contained within it. We can see this behavior in operation by adding a border to the ul element in the previous example:

```
ul {margin-bottom: 15px; border: 1px solid;}
li {margin-top: 10px; margin-bottom: 20px;}
h1 {margin-top: 28px;}
```

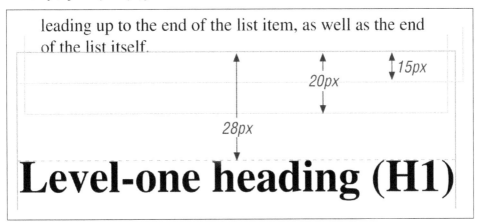

Figure 25. Collapsing in detail

With this change, the bottom margin of the li element is now placed inside its parent element (the ul). Therefore, the only margin collapsing that takes place is between the ul and the h1, as illustrated in Figure 26.

- A list item.

- Another list item.

A Heading-1

Figure 26. Collapsing (or not) with borders added to the mix

Negative Margins and Collapsing

Negative margins do have an impact on vertical formatting, and they affect how margins are collapsed. If negative vertical margins are set, then the browser should take the absolute maximum of both margins. The absolute value of the negative margin is then subtracted from the positive margin. In other words, the negative is added to the positive, and the resulting value is the distance between the elements. Figure 27 provides two concrete examples.

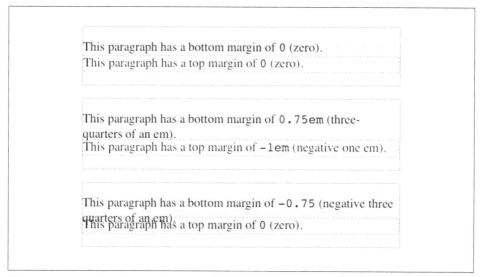

Figure 27. Examples of negative vertical margins

Notice the "pulling" effect of negative top and bottom margins. This is really no different from the way that negative horizontal margins cause an element to push outside of its parent. Consider:

```
p.neg {margin-top: -50px; margin-right: 10px;
    margin-left: 10px; margin-bottom: 0;
    border: 3px solid gray;}

<div style="width: 420px; background-color: silver; padding: 10px;
        margin-top: 50px; border: 1px solid;">
    <p class="neg">
        A paragraph.
    </p>

    A div.

</div>
```

As we see in Figure 28, the paragraph has simply been pulled upward by its negative top margin. Note that the content of the div that follows the paragraph in the markup has also been pulled upward 50 pixels. In fact, every bit of normal-flow content that follows the paragraph is also pulled upward 50 pixels.

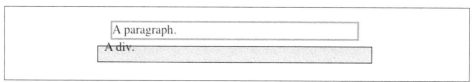

Figure 28. The effects of a negative top margin

Now compare the following markup to the situation shown in Figure 29:

```
p.neg {margin-bottom: -50px; margin-right: 10px;
    margin-left: 10px; margin-top: 0;
    border: 3px solid gray;}

<div style="width: 420px; margin-top: 50px;">
    <p class="neg">
        A paragraph.
    </p>
</div>
<p>
    The next paragraph.
</p>
```

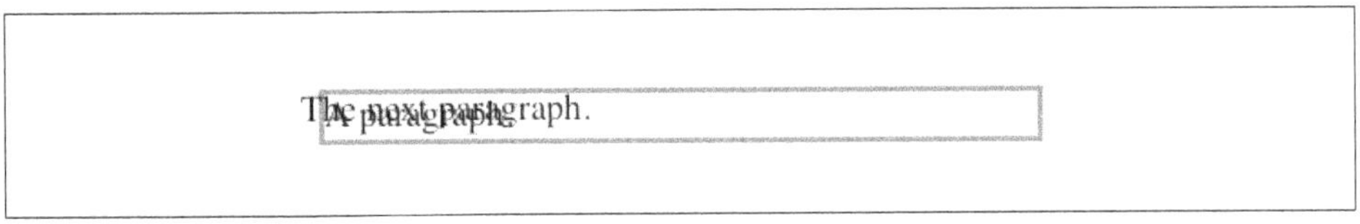

Figure 29. The effects of a negative bottom margin

What's really happening in Figure 29 is that the elements following the div are placed according to the location of the bottom of the div. As you can see, the end of the div is actually above the visual bottom of its child paragraph. The next element after the div is the appropriate distance from the bottom of the div. This is expected, given the rules we saw.

Now let's consider an example where the margins of a list item, an unordered list, and a paragraph are all collapsed. In this case, the unordered list and paragraph are assigned negative margins:

```
li {margin-bottom: 20px;}
ul {margin-bottom: -15px;}
h1 {margin-top: -18px;}
```

The larger of the two negative margins (-18px) is added to the largest positive margin (20px), yielding 20px - 18px = 2px. Thus, there are only two pixels between the bottom of the list item's content and the top of the h1's content, as we can see in Figure 30.

When elements overlap each other due to negative margins, it's hard to tell which elements are on top. You may also have noticed that none of the examples in this section use background colors. If they did, the background color of a following element might overwrite their content. This is expected behavior, since browsers usually render elements in order from beginning to end, so a normal-flow element that comes later in the document can be expected to overwrite an earlier element, assuming the two end up overlapping.

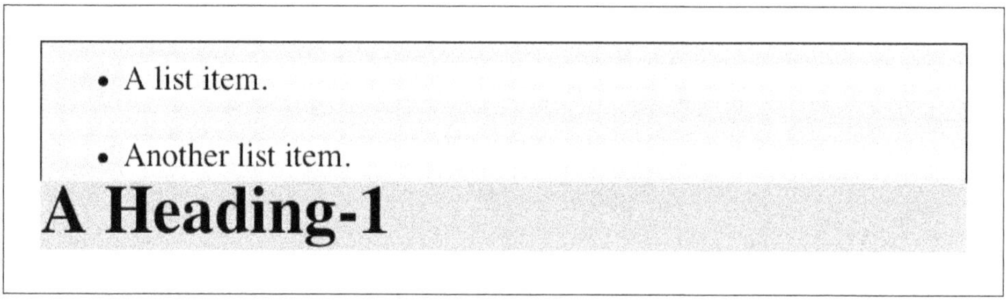

Figure 30. Collapsing margins and negative margins, in detail

List Items

List items have a few special rules of their own. They are typically preceded by a marker, such as a small dot or a number. This marker isn't actually part of the list item's content area, so effects like those illustrated in Figure 31 are common.

CSS1 said very little about the placement and effects of these markers with regard to the layout of a document. CSS2 introduced properties specifically designed to address this issue, such as `marker-offset`. However, a lack of implementations and changes in thinking caused this to be dropped from CSS2.1, and work is being done to reintroduce the idea (if not the specific syntax) to CSS. Accordingly, the placement of markers is largely beyond the control of authors, at least as of this writing.

The marker attached to a list item element can be either outside the content of the list item or treated as an inline marker at the beginning of the content, depending on the value of the property `list-style-position`. If the marker is brought inside, then the list item will interact with its neighbors exactly like a block-level element, as illustrated in Figure 32.

If the marker stays outside the content, then it is placed some distance from the left content edge of the content (in left-to-right languages). No matter how the list's styles are altered, the marker stays the same distance from the content edge. Occasionally, the markers may be pushed outside of the list element itself, as we can see in Figure 32.

Remember that list-item boxes define containing blocks for their ancestor boxes, just like regular block boxes.

Inline Elements

After block-level elements, inline elements are the most common. Setting box properties for inline elements takes us into more interesting territory than we've been so far. Some good examples of inline elements are the em tag and the a tag, both of which are nonreplaced elements, and images, which are replaced elements.

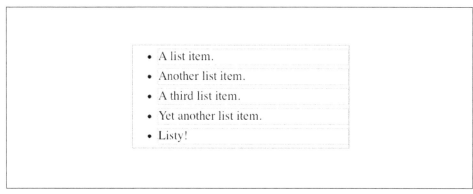

Figure 31. The content of list items

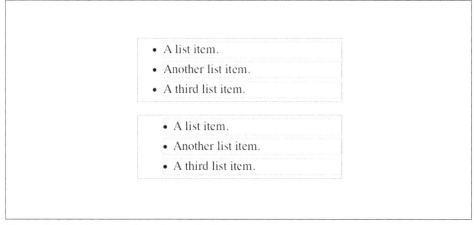

Figure 32. Markers inside and outside the list

Note that none of the behavior described in this section applies to table elements. CSS2 introduced new properties and behaviors for handling tables and table content, and these elements behave in ways fairly distinct from either block-level or inline formatting. Table styling is beyond the scope of this book, as it's surprisingly complicated and exists rather in a world of its own.

Nonreplaced and replaced elements are treated somewhat differently in the inline context, and we'll look at each in turn as we explore the construction of inline elements.

Line Layout

First, you need to understand how inline content is laid out. It isn't as simple and straightforward as block-level elements, which just generate block boxes and usually don't allow anything to coexist with them. By contrast, look *inside* a block-level element, such as a paragraph. You may well ask, how did all those lines of text get there? What controls their arrangement? How can I affect it?

In order to understand how lines are generated, first consider the case of an element containing one very long line of text, as shown in Figure 33. Note that we've put a border around the line by wrapping the entire line in a span element and then assigning it a border style:

```
span {border: 1px dashed black;}
```

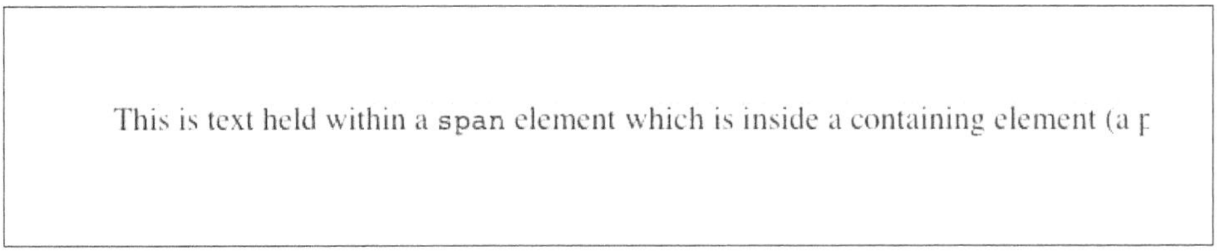

This is text held within a span element which is inside a containing element (a p

Figure 33. A single-line inline element

Figure 33 shows the simplest case of an inline element contained by a block-level element. It's no different in its way than a paragraph with two words in it. The only differences are that, in Figure 34, we have a few dozen words and most paragraphs don't contain an explicit inline element such as span.

In order to get from this simplified state to something more familiar, all we have to do is determine how wide the element should be, and then break up the line so that the resulting pieces will fit into the content width of the element. Therefore, we arrive at the state shown in Figure 34.

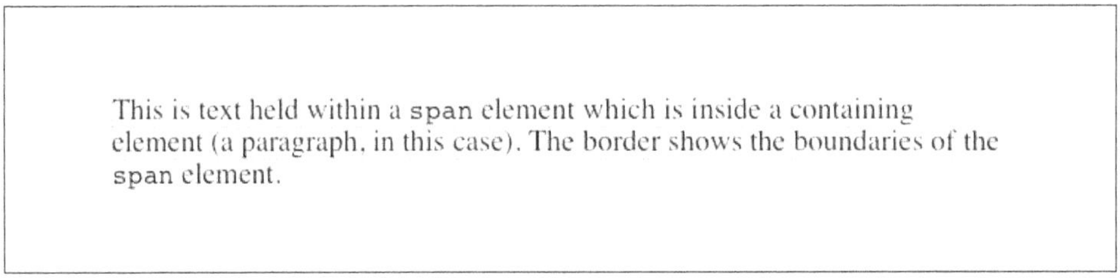

This is text held within a span element which is inside a containing element (a paragraph, in this case). The border shows the boundaries of the span element.

Figure 34. A multiple-line inline element

Nothing has really changed. All we did was take the single line and break it into pieces, and then stack those pieces on top of each other.

In Figure 34, the borders for each line of text also happen to coincide with the top and bottom of each line. This is true only because no padding has been set for the inline text. Notice that the borders actually overlap each other slightly; for example, the bottom border of the first line is just below the top border of the second line. This is because the border is actually drawn on the next pixel (assuming you're using a monitor) to the *outside* of each line. Since the lines are touching each other, their borders will overlap as shown in Figure 34.

If we alter the span styles to have a background color, the actual placement of the lines becomes quite clear. Consider Figure 35, which contains four paragraphs, each with a different value of `text-align` and each having the backgrounds of its lines <span class="keep-together">filled in.</span>

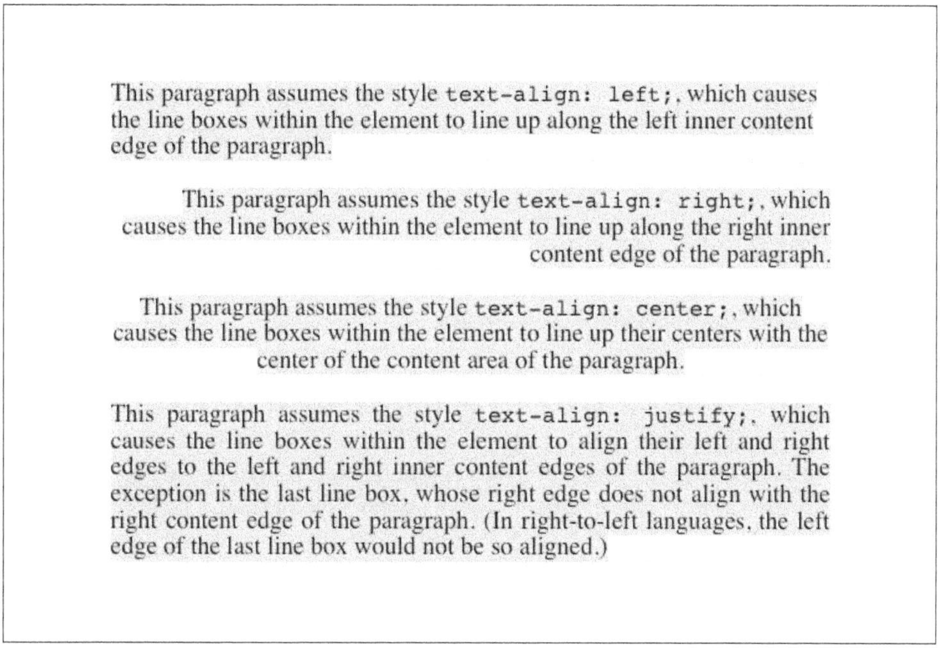

This paragraph assumes the style `text-align: left;`, which causes the line boxes within the element to line up along the left inner content edge of the paragraph.

This paragraph assumes the style `text-align: right;`, which causes the line boxes within the element to line up along the right inner content edge of the paragraph.

This paragraph assumes the style `text-align: center;`, which causes the line boxes within the element to line up their centers with the center of the content area of the paragraph.

This paragraph assumes the style `text-align: justify;`, which causes the line boxes within the element to align their left and right edges to the left and right inner content edges of the paragraph. The exception is the last line box, whose right edge does not align with the right content edge of the paragraph. (In right-to-left languages, the left edge of the last line box would not be so aligned.)

Figure 35. Showing lines in different alignments

As we can see, not every line reaches to the edge of its parent paragraph's content area, which has been denoted with a dotted gray border. For the left-aligned paragraph, the lines are all pushed flush against the left content edge of the paragraph, and the end of each line happens wherever the line is broken. The reverse is true for the right-aligned paragraph. For the centered paragraph, the centers of the lines are aligned with the center of the paragraph.

In the last case, where the value of `text-align` is `justify`, each line is forced to be as wide as the paragraph's content area so that the line's edges touch the content edges of the paragraph. The difference between the natural length of the line and the width of the paragraph is made up by altering the spacing between letters and words in each line. Therefore, the value of `word-spacing` can be overridden when the text is justified. (The value of `letter-spacing` cannot be overridden if it is a length value.)

That pretty well covers how lines are generated in the simplest cases. As you're about to see, however, the inline formatting model is far from simple.

Basic Terms and Concepts

Before we go any further, let's review some basic terms of inline layout, which will be crucial in navigating the following sections:

Anonymous text

This is any string of characters that is not contained within an inline element. Thus, in the markup `<p> I'm <em>so</em> happy!</p>`, the sequences " I'm " and " happy!" are anonymous text. Note that the spaces are part of the text since a space is a character like any other.

Em box

This is defined in the given font, otherwise known as the character box. Actual glyphs can be taller or shorter than their em boxes. In CSS, the value of `font-size` determines the height of each em box.

Content area

In nonreplaced elements, the content area can be one of two things, and the CSS specification allows user agents to choose which one. The content area can be the box described by the em boxes of every character in the element, strung together; or it can be the box described by the character glyphs in the element. In this book, I use the em box definition for simplicity's sake. In replaced elements, the content area is the intrinsic height of the element plus any margins, borders, or padding.

Leading

Leading is the difference between the values of `font-size` and `line-height`. This difference is actually divided in half and is applied equally to the top and bottom of the content area. These additions to the content area are called, not surprisingly, *half-leading*. Leading is applied only to nonreplaced elements.

Inline box

This is the box described by the addition of the leading to the content area. For nonreplaced elements, the height of the inline box of an element will be exactly equal to the value for `line-height`. For replaced elements, the height of the inline box of an element will be exactly equal to the content area, since leading is not applied to replaced elements.

Line box

This is the shortest box that bounds the highest and lowest points of the inline boxes that are found in the line. In other words, the top edge of the line box is placed along the top of the highest inline box top, and the bottom of the line box is placed along the bottom of the lowest inline box bottom.

CSS also contains a set of behaviors and useful concepts that fall outside of the above list of terms and definitions:

- The content area is analogous to the content box of a block box.
- The background of an inline element is applied to the content area plus any padding.
- Any border on an inline element surrounds the content area plus any padding and border.
- Padding, borders, and margins on nonreplaced elements have no vertical effect on inline elements or the boxes they generate; that is, they do *not* affect the height of an element's inline box (and thus the line box that contains the element).
- Margins and borders on replaced elements *do* affect the height of the inline box for that element and, by implication, the height of the line box for the line that contains the element.

One more thing to note: inline boxes are vertically aligned within the line according to their values for the property `vertical-align`.

Before moving on, let's look at a step-by-step process for constructing a line box, which you can use to see how the various pieces of the line fit together to determine its height.

Determine the height of the inline box for each element in the line by following these steps:

1. Find the values of `font-size` and `line-height` for each inline nonreplaced element and text that is not part of a descendant inline element and combine them. This is done by subtracting the `font-size` from the `line-height`, which yields the leading for the box. The leading is split in half and applied to the top and bottom of each em box.

2. Find the values of `height`, `margin-top`, `margin-bottom`, `padding-top`, `padding-bottom`, `border-top-width`, and `border-bottom-width` for each replaced element and add them together.

3. Figure out, for each content area, how much of it is above the baseline for the overall line and how much of it is below the baseline. This is not an easy task: you must know the position of the baseline for each element and piece of anonymous text and the baseline of the line itself, and then line them all up. In addition, the bottom edge of a replaced element sits on the baseline for the overall line.

4. Determine the vertical offset of any elements that have been given a value for `vertical-align`. This will tell you how far up or down that element's inline box will be moved, and it will change how much of the element is above or below the baseline.

5. Now that you know where all of the inline boxes have come to rest, calculate the final line box height. To do so, just add the distance between the baseline and the highest inline box top to the distance between the baseline and the lowest inline box bottom.

Let's consider the whole process in detail, which is the key to intelligently styling inline content.

Inline Formatting

First, know that all elements have a `line-height`, whether it's explicitly declared or not. This value greatly influences the way inline elements are displayed, so let's give it due attention.

Now let's establish how to determine the height of a line. A line's height (or the height of the line box) is determined by the height of its constituent elements and other content, such as text. It's important to understand that `line-height` actually affects inline elements and other inline content, *not* block-level elements—at least, not directly. We can set a `line-height` value for a block-level element, but the value will have a visual impact only as it's applied to inline content within that block-level element. Consider the following empty paragraph, for example:

```
<p style="line-height: 0.25em;"></p>
```

Without content, the paragraph won't have anything to display, so we won't see anything. The fact that this paragraph has a `line-height` of any value—be it `0.25em` or `25in`—makes no difference without some content to create a line box.

We can certainly set a `line-height` value for a block-level element and have that apply to all of the content within the block, whether or not the content is contained in any inline elements. In a certain sense, then, each line of text contained within a block-level element is its own inline element, whether or not it's surrounded by tags. If you like, picture a fictional tag sequence like this:

```
<p>
<line>This is a paragraph with a number of</line>
<line>lines of text which make up the</line>
<line>contents.</line>
</p>
```

Even though the `line` tags don't actually exist, the paragraph behaves as if they did—each line of text inherits styles from the paragraph. Therefore, you only bother to create `line-height` rules for block-level elements so you don't have to explicitly declare a `line-height` for all of their inline elements, fictional or otherwise.

The fictional `line` element actually clarifies the behavior that results from setting `line-height` on a block-level element. According to the CSS specification, declaring `line-height` on a block-level element sets a *minimum* line box height for the content of that block-level element. Thus, declaring `p.spacious {line-height: 24pt;}` means that the *minimum* heights for each line box is 24 points. Technically, content can inherit this line height only if an inline element does so. Most text isn't contained by an inline element. Therefore, if you pretend that each line is contained by the fictional `line` element, the model works out very nicely.

Inline Nonreplaced Elements

Building on your formatting knowledge, let's move on to the construction of lines that contain only nonreplaced elements (or anonymous text). Then you'll be in a good position to understand the differences between nonreplaced and replaced elements in inline layout.

Building the Boxes

First, for an inline nonreplaced element or piece of anonymous text, the value of `font-size` determines the height of the content area. If an inline element has a `font-size` of 15px, then the content area's height is 15 pixels because all of the em boxes in the element are 15 pixels tall, as illustrated in Figure 36.

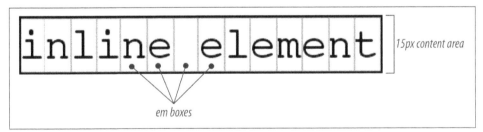

Figure 36. Em boxes determine content area height

The next thing to consider is the value of `line-height` for the element, and the difference between it and the value of `font-size`. If an inline nonreplaced element has a `font-size` of 15px and a `line-height` of 21px, then the difference is six pixels. The user agent splits the six pixels in half and applies half to the top and half to the bottom of the content area, which yields the inline box. This process is illustrated in Figure 37.

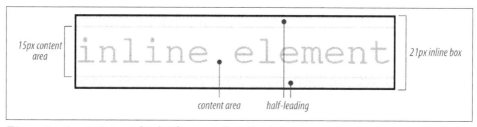

Figure 37. Content area plus leading equals inline box

Let's assume that the following is true:

```
<p style="font-size: 12px; line-height: 12px;">
This is text, <em>some of which is emphasized</em>, plus other text<br>
which is <strong style="font-size: 24px;">strongly emphasized</strong>
and which is<br>
larger than the surrounding text.
</p>
```

In this example, most of the text has a font-size of 12px, while the text in one inline nonreplaced element has a size of 24px. However, *all* of the text has a line-height of 12px since line-height is an inherited property. Therefore, the strong element's line-height is also 12px.

Thus, for each piece of text where both the font-size and line-height are 12px, the content height does not change (since the difference between 12px and 12px is zero), so the inline box is 12 pixels high. For the strong text, however, the difference between line-height and font-size is -12px. This is divided in half to determine the half-leading (-6px), and the half-leading is added to both the top and bottom of the content height to arrive at an inline box. Since we're adding a negative number in both cases, the inline box ends up being 12 pixels tall. The 12-pixel inline box is centered vertically within the 24-pixel content height of the element, so the inline box is actually smaller than the content area.

So far, it sounds like we've done the same thing to each bit of text, and that all the inline boxes are the same size, but that's not quite true. The inline boxes in the second line, although they're the same size, don't actually line up because the text is all baseline-aligned (see Figure 38).

Since inline boxes determine the height of the overall line box, their placement with respect to each other is critical. The line box is defined as the distance from the top of the highest inline box in the line to the bottom of the lowest inline box, and the top of each line box butts up against the bottom of the line box for the preceding line. The result shown in Figure 38 gives us the paragraph shown in Figure 39.

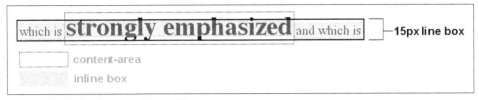

Figure 38. Inline boxes within a line

This is text, *some of which is emphasized*, plus other text
which is **strongly emphasized** and which is
larger than the surrounding text.

Figure 39. Line boxes within a paragraph

As we can see in Figure 39, the middle line is taller than the other two, but it still isn't big enough to contain all of the text within it. The anonymous text's inline box determines the bottom of the line box, while the top of the strong element's inline box sets the top of the line box. Because that inline box's top is inside the element's content area, the contents of the element spill outside the line box and actually overlap other line boxes. The result is that the lines of text look irregular.

In just a bit, we'll explore ways to cope with this behavior and methods for achieving consistent baseline spacing.

Vertical Alignment

If we change the vertical alignment of the inline boxes, the same height determination principles apply. Suppose that we give the strong element a vertical alignment of 4px:

```
<p style="font-size: 12px; line-height: 12px;">
This is text, <em>some of which is emphasized</em>, plus other text<br>
which is <strong style="font-size: 24px; vertical-align: 4px;">strongly
emphasized</strong> and that is<br>
larger than the surrounding text.
</p>
```

That small change raises the strong element four pixels, which pushes up both its content area and its inline box. Because the strong element's inline box top was already the highest in the line, this change in vertical alignment also pushes the top of the line box upward by four pixels, as shown in Figure 40.

Figure 40. Vertical alignment affects line box height

Let's consider another situation. Here, we have another inline element in the same line as the strong text, and its alignment is other than the baseline:

```
<p style="font-size: 12px; line-height: 12px;">
This is text, <em>some of which is emphasized</em>,<br>
plus other text that is <strong style="font-size: 24px;">strong</strong>
 and <span style="vertical-align: top;">tall</span> and is<br>
larger than the surrounding text.
</p>
```

Now we have the same result as in our earlier example, where the middle line box is taller than the other line boxes. However, notice how the "tall" text is aligned in Figure 41.

Figure 41. Aligning an inline element to the line box

In this case, the top of the "tall" text's inline box is aligned with the top of the line box. Since the "tall" text has equal values for font-size and line-height, the content height and inline box are the same. However, consider this:

```
<p style="font-size: 12px; line-height: 12px;">
This is text, <em>some of which is emphasized</em>,<br>
plus other text that is <strong style="font-size: 24px;">strong</strong>
 and <span style="vertical-align: top; line-height: 2px;">tall</span> and is<br>
```

```
larger than the surrounding text.
</p>
```

Since the line-height for the "tall" text is less than its font-size, the inline box for that element is smaller than its content area. This tiny fact changes the placement of the text itself since the top of its inline box must be aligned with the top of the line box for its line. Thus, we get the result shown in Figure 42.

On the other hand, we could set the "tall" text to have a line-height that is actually bigger than its font-size. For example:

```
<p style="font-size: 12px; line-height: 12px;">
This is text, <em>some of which is emphasized</em>, plus other text<br>
that is <strong style="font-size: 24px;">strong</strong>
and <span style="vertical-align: top; line-height: 18px;">tall</span>
and that is<br>
larger than the surrounding text.
</p>
```

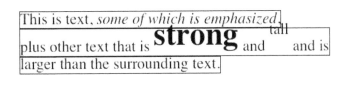

Figure 42. Text protruding from the line box (again)

Since we've given the "tall" text a line-height of 18px, the difference between line-height and font-size is six pixels. The half-leading of three pixels is added to the content area and results in an inline box that is 18 pixels tall. The top of this inline box aligns with the top of the line box. Similarly, the vertical-align value bottom will align the bottom of an inline element's inline box with the bottom of the line box.

In relation to the terms we've been using in this chapter, the effects of the assorted keyword values of vertical-align are:

top
    Aligns the top of the element's inline box with the top of the containing line box

bottom
    Aligns the bottom of the element's inline box with the bottom of the containing line box

text-top
    Aligns the top of the element's inline box with the top of the parent's content area

`text-bottom`

Aligns the bottom of the element's inline box with the bottom of the parent's content area

`middle`

Aligns the vertical midpoint of the element's inline box with `0.5ex` above the baseline of the parent

`super`

Moves the content area and inline box of the element upward. The distance is not specified and may vary by user agent

`sub`

The same as super, except the element is moved downward instead of upward

`<percentage>`

Shifts the element up or down the distance defined by taking the declared percentage of the element's value for `line-height`

Managing the line-height

In previous sections, we saw that changing the `line-height` of an inline element can cause text from one line to overlap another. In each case, though, the changes were made to individual elements. So how can we affect the `line-height` of elements in a more general way in order to keep content from overlapping?

One way to do this is to use the `em` unit in conjunction with an element whose `font-size` has changed. For example:

```
p {line-height: 1em;}
big {font-size: 250%; line-height: 1em;}

<p>
Not only does this paragraph have "normal" text, but it also<br>
contains a line in which <big>some big text</big> is found.<br>
This large text helps illustrate our point.
</p>
```

By setting a `line-height` for the `big` element, we increase the overall height of the line box, providing enough room to display the big element without overlapping any other text and without changing the `line-height` of all lines in the paragraph. We use a value of `1em` so that the `line-height` for the `big` element will be set to the same size as `big`'s font-size. Remember, `line-height` is set in relation to the `font-size` of the element itself, not the parent element. The results are shown in Figure 43.

Figure 43. Assigning the line-height property to inline elements

Make sure you really understand the previous sections, because things will get trickier when we try to add borders. Let's say we want to put five-pixel borders around any hyperlink:

```
a:link {border: 5px solid blue;}
```

If we don't set a large enough `line-height` to accommodate the border, it will be in danger of overwriting other lines. We could increase the size of the inline box for unvisited links using `line-height`, as we did for the `big` element in the earlier example; in this case, we'd just need to make the value of `line-height` 10 pixels larger than the value of font-size for those links. However, that will be difficult if we don't actually know the size of the font in pixels.

Another solution is to increase the `line-height` of the paragraph. This will affect every line in the entire element, not just the line in which the bordered hyperlink appears:

```
p {line-height: 1.8em;}
a:link {border: 5px solid blue;}
```

Because there is extra space added above and below each line, the border around the hyperlink doesn't impinge on any other line, as we can see in Figure 44.

This approach works here, of course, because all of the text is the same size. If there were other elements in the line that changed the height of the line box, our border situation might also change. Consider the following:

```
p {font-size: 14px; line-height: 24px;}
a:link {border: 5px solid blue;}
big {font-size: 150%; line-height: 1.5em;}
```

Given these rules, the height of the inline box of a `big` element within a paragraph will be 31.5 pixels ($14 \times 1.5 \times 1.5$), and that will also be the height of the line box. In order to keep baseline spacing consistent, we must make the p element's `line-height` equal to or greater than 32px.

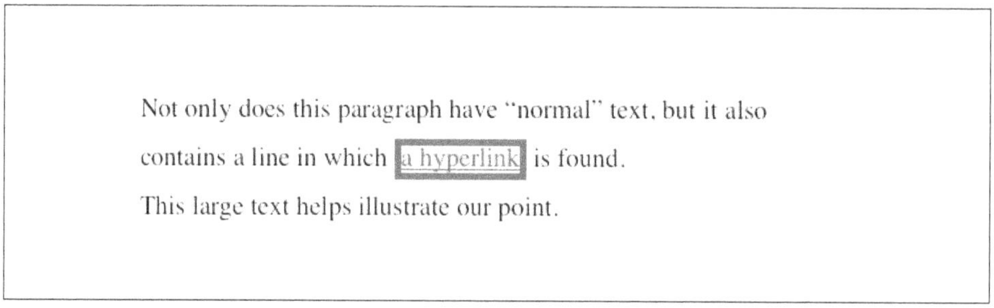

Not only does this paragraph have "normal" text, but it also

contains a line in which a hyperlink is found.

This large text helps illustrate our point.

Figure 44. Increasing line-height to leave room for inline borders

Baselines and line heights

The actual height of each line box depends on the way its component elements line up with one another. This alignment tends to depend very much on where the baseline falls within each element (or piece of anonymous text) because that location determines how the inline boxes are arranged. The placement of the baseline within each em box is different for every font. This information is built into the font files and cannot be altered by any means other than directly editing the font files.

Thus, consistent baseline spacing tends to be more of an art than a science. If you declare all of your font sizes and line heights using a single unit, such as ems, then you have a reliable chance of consistent baseline spacing. If you mix units, however, that feat becomes a great deal more difficult, if not impossible. As of this writing, there are proposals for properties that would let authors enforce consistent baseline spacing regardless of the inline content, which would greatly simplify certain aspects of online typography. None of these proposed properties have been implemented though, which makes their adoption a distant hope at best.

Scaling Line Heights

The best way to set line-height, as it turns out, is to use a raw number as the value. This method is the best because the number becomes the scaling factor, and that factor is an inherited, not a computed, value. Let's say we want the line-height`s of all elements in a document to be one and a half times their `font-size. We would declare:

```
body {line-height: 1.5;}
```

This scaling factor of 1.5 is passed down from element to element, and, at each level, the factor is used as a multiplier of the font-size of each element. Therefore, the following markup would be displayed as shown in Figure 45:

```
p {font-size: 15px; line-height: 1.5;}
small {font-size: 66%;}
big {font-size: 200%;}
```

```
<p>This paragraph has a line-height of 1.5 times its font-size. In addition,
any elements within it <small>such as this small element</small> also have
line-heights 1.5 times their font-size...and that includes <big>this big
element right here</big>. By using a scaling factor, line-heights scale
to match the font-size of any element.</p>
```

In this example, the line height for the small element turns out to be 15 pixels, and for the big element, it's 45 pixels. (These numbers may seem excessive, but they're in keeping with the overall page design.) Of course, if we don't want our big text to generate too much extra leading, we can give it a line-height value, which will override the inherited scaling factor:

```
p {font-size: 15px; line-height: 1.5;}
small {font-size: 66%;}
big {font-size: 200%; line-height: 1em;}
```

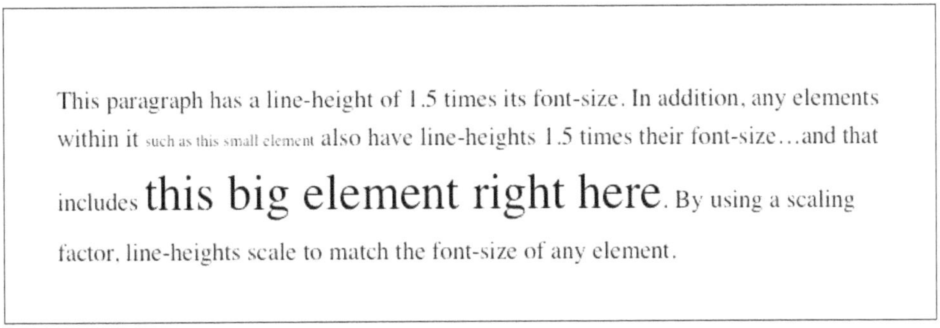

This paragraph has a line-height of 1.5 times its font-size. In addition, any elements within it such as this small element also have line-heights 1.5 times their font-size…and that includes this big element right here. By using a scaling factor, line-heights scale to match the font-size of any element.

Figure 45. Using a scaling factor for line-height

Another solution—possibly the simplest of all—is to set the styles such that lines are no taller than absolutely necessary to hold their content. This is where we might use a line-height of 1.0. This value will multiply itself by every font-size to get the same value as the font-size of every element. Thus, for every element, the inline box will be the same as the content area, which will mean the absolute minimum size necessary is used to contain the content area of each element.

Most fonts still display a little bit of space between the lines of character glyphs because characters are usually smaller than their em boxes. The exception is script ("cursive") fonts, where character glyphs are usually *larger* than their em boxes.

Adding Box Properties

As you're aware from previous discussions, padding, margins, and borders may all be applied to inline nonreplaced elements. These aspects of the inline element do not influence the height of the line box at all. If you were to apply some borders to a span element without any margins or padding, you'd get results such as those shown in Figure 46.

The border edge of inline elements is controlled by the `font-size`, not the `line-height`. In other words, if a `span` element has a `font-size` of 12px and a `line-height` of 36px, its content area is 12px high, and the border will surround that content area.

Alternatively, we can assign padding to the inline element, which will push the borders away from the text itself:

```
span {padding: 4px;}
```

Note that this padding does not alter the actual shape of the content height, and so it will not affect the height of the inline box for this element. Similarly, adding borders to an inline element will not affect the way line boxes are generated and laid out, as illustrated in Figure 47.

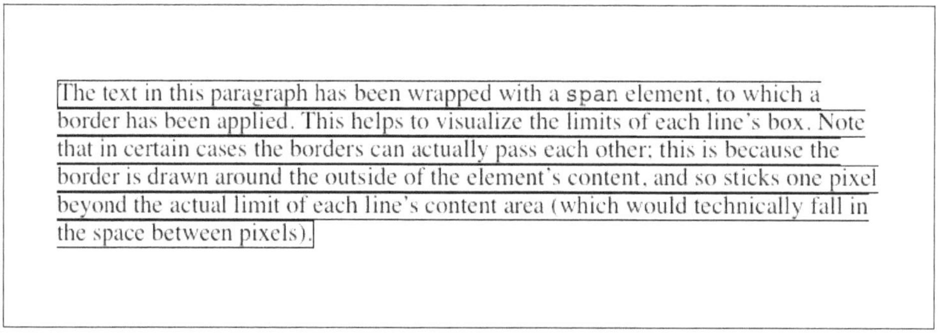

Figure 46. Inline borders and line-box layout

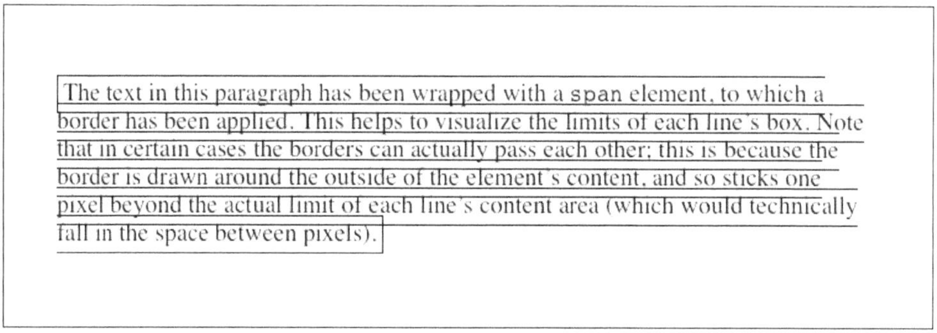

Figure 47. Padding and borders do not alter line-height

As for margins, they do not, practically speaking, apply to the top and bottom of an inline nonreplaced element, as they don't affect the height of the line box. The ends of the element are another story.

Recall the idea that an inline element is basically laid out as a single line and then broken up into pieces. So, if we apply margins to an inline element, those margins will appear at its beginning and end: these are the left and right margins, respectively.

Padding also appears at the edges. Thus, although padding and margins (and borders) do not affect line heights, they can still affect the layout of an element's content by pushing text away from its ends. In fact, negative left and right margins can pull text closer to the inline element, or even cause overlap, as Figure 48 shows.

Think of an inline element as a strip of paper with some plastic surrounding it. Displaying the inline element on multiple lines is like slicing up the strip into smaller strips. However, no extra plastic is added to each smaller strip. The only plastic is that which was on the strip to begin with, so it appears only at the beginning and end of the original ends of the paper strip (the inline element). At least, that's the default behavior, but as we'll soon see, there is another option.

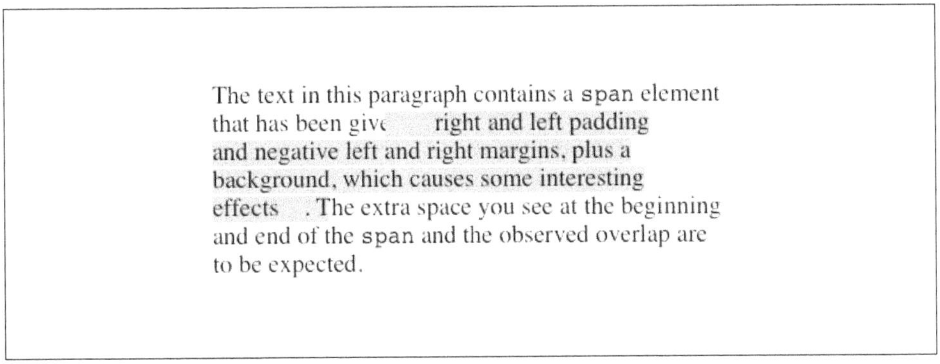

The text in this paragraph contains a span element that has been give   right and left padding and negative left and right margins, plus a background, which causes some interesting effects   . The extra space you see at the beginning and end of the span and the observed overlap are to be expected.

Figure 48. Padding and margins on the ends of an inline element

So, what happens when an inline element has a background and enough padding to cause the lines' backgrounds to overlap? Take the following situation as an example:

```
p {font-size: 15px; line-height: 1em;}
p span {background: #FAA; padding-top: 10px; padding-bottom: 10px;}
```

All of the text within the span element will have a content area 15 pixels tall, and we've applied 10 pixels of padding to the top and bottom of each content area. The extra pixels won't increase the height of the line box, which would be fine, except there is a background color. Thus, we get the result shown in Figure 49.

CSS 2.1 explicitly states that the line boxes are drawn in document order: "This will cause the borders on subsequent lines to paint over the borders and text of previous lines." The same principle applies to backgrounds as well, as Figure 49 shows. CSS2, on the other hand, allowed user agents "to 'clip' the border and padding areas (i.e., not render them)." Therefore, the results may depend greatly on which specification the user agent follows.

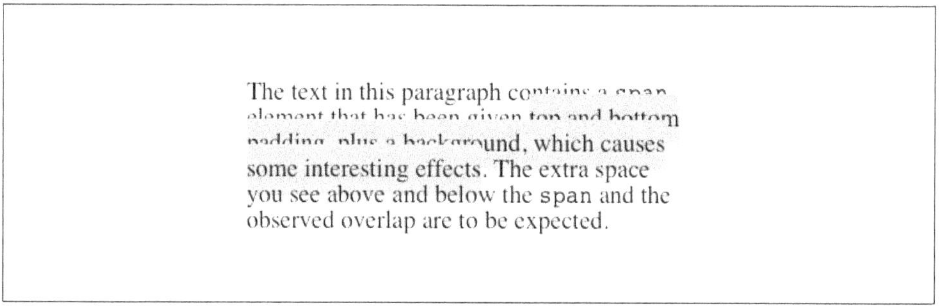

The text in this paragraph contains a span element that has been given top and bottom padding, plus a background, which causes some interesting effects. The extra space you see above and below the span and the observed overlap are to be expected.

Figure 49. Overlapping inline backgrounds

Changing Breaking Behavior

In the previous section, we saw that when an inline nonreplaced element is broken across multiple lines, it's treated as if it were one long single-line element that's sliced into smaller boxes, one slice per line break. That's actually just the default behavior, and it can be changed via the property `box-decoration-break`.

box-decoration-break

Values:	`slice|clone|inherit`
Initial value:	`slice`
Applies to:	All elements
Inherited:	No
Computed value:	As specified

The default value, `slice`, is what we saw in the previous section. The other value, `clone`, causes each fragment of the element to be drawn as if it were a standalone box. What does that mean? Compare the two examples in Figure 50, in which exactly the same markup and styles are treated as either sliced or cloned.

Many of the differences are pretty apparent, but a few are perhaps more subtle. Among the obvious effects are the application of padding to each element's fragment, including at the ends where the linebreaks occurred. Similarly, the border is drawn around each fragment individually, instead of being broken up.

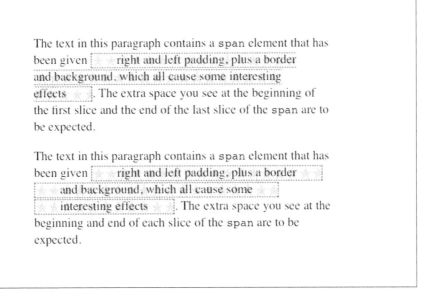

Figure 50. Sliced and cloned inline fragments

More subtly, notice how the background-image positioning changes between the two. In the sliced version, background images are sliced along with everything else, meaning that only one of the fragments contains the origin image. In the cloned version, however, each background acts as its own copy, so each has its own origin image. This means, for example, that even if we have a nonrepeated background image, it will appear once in each fragment instead of only in one fragment.

The box-decoration-break property will most often be used with inline boxes, but it actually applies in any situation where there's a break in an element—for example, when a page break interrupts an element in paged media. In such a case, each fragment is a separate slice. If we set box-decoration-break: clone, then each box fragment will be treated as a copy when it comes to borders, padding, backgrounds, and so on. The same holds true in multicolumn layout: if an element is split by a column break, the value of box-decoration-break will affect how it is rendered.

Glyphs Versus Content Area

Even in cases where you try to keep inline nonreplaced element backgrounds from overlapping, it can still happen, depending on which font is in use. The problem lies in the difference between a font's em box and its character glyphs. Most fonts, as it turns out, don't have em boxes whose heights match the character glyphs.

That may sound very abstract, but it has practical consequences. In CSS2.1, we find the following: "the height of the content area should be based on the font, but this specification does not specify how. A user agent may…use the em box or the maximum ascender and descender of the font. (The latter would ensure that glyphs with parts above or below the em box still fall within the content area, but leads to differently sized boxes for different fonts.)"

In other words, the "painting area" of an inline nonreplaced element is left to the user agent. If a user agent takes the em box to be the height of the content area, then the background of an inline nonreplaced element will be equal to the height of the em box (which is the value of font-size). If a user agent uses the maximum ascender and descender of the font, then the background may be taller or shorter than the em box. Therefore, you could give an inline nonreplaced element a line-height of 1em and still have its background overlap the content of other lines.

Inline Replaced Elements

Inline replaced elements, such as images, are assumed to have an intrinsic height and width; for example, an image will be a certain number of pixels high and wide. Therefore, a replaced element with an intrinsic height can cause a line box to become taller than normal. This does *not* change the value of line-height for any element in the line, *including the replaced element itself*. Instead, the line box is simply made tall enough to accommodate the replaced element, plus any box properties. In other words, the entirety of the replaced element—content, margins, borders, and padding —is used to define the element's inline box. The following styles lead to one such example, as shown in Figure 51:

```
p {font-size: 15px; line-height: 18px;}
img {height: 30px; margin: 0; padding: 0; border: none;}
```

Despite all the blank space, the effective value of line-height has not changed, either for the paragraph or the image itself. line-height simply has no effect on the image's inline box. Because the image in Figure 51 has no padding, margins, or borders, its inline box is equivalent to its content area, which is, in this case, 30 pixels tall.

Nonetheless, an inline replaced element still has a value for line-height. Why? In the most common case, it needs the value in order to correctly position the element if it's been vertically aligned. Recall that, for example, percentage values for vertical-align are calculated with respect to an element's line-height. Thus:

```
p {font-size: 15px; line-height: 18px;}
img {vertical-align: 50%;}

<p>the image in this sentence <img src="test.gif" alt="test image">
will be raised 9 pixels.</p>
```

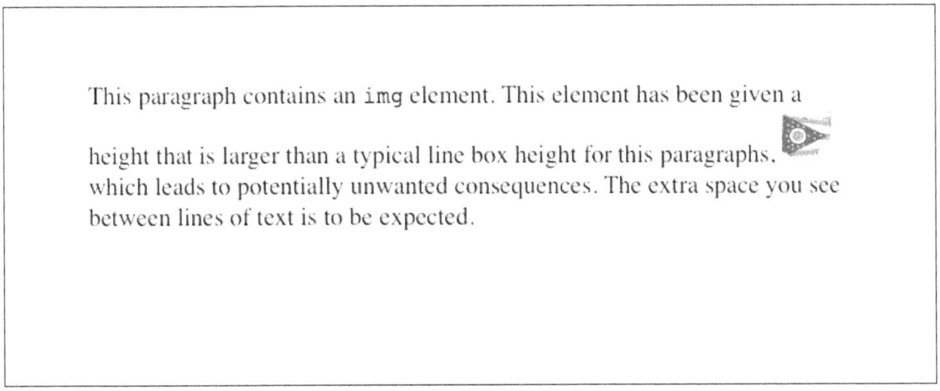

This paragraph contains an `img` element. This element has been given a
height that is larger than a typical line box height for this paragraphs,
which leads to potentially unwanted consequences. The extra space you see
between lines of text is to be expected.

Figure 51. Replaced elements can increase the height of the line box but not the value of line-height

The inherited value of `line-height` causes the image to be raised nine pixels instead of some other number. Without a value for `line-height`, it wouldn't be possible to perform percentage-value vertical alignments. The height of the image itself has no relevance when it comes to vertical alignment; the value of `line-height` is all that matters.

However, for other replaced elements, it might be important to pass on a `line-height` value to descendant elements within that replaced element. An example would be an SVG image, which uses CSS to style any text found within the image.

Adding Box Properties

After everything we've just been through, applying margins, borders, and padding to inline replaced elements almost seems simple.

Padding and borders are applied to replaced elements as usual; padding inserts space around the actual content and the border surrounds the padding. What's unusual about the process is that these two things actually influence the height of the line box because they are part of the inline box of an inline replaced element (unlike inline nonreplaced elements). Consider Figure 52, which results from the following styles:

```
img {height: 50px; width: 50px;}
img.one {margin: 0; padding: 0; border: 3px dotted;}
img.two {margin: 10px; padding: 10px; border: 3px solid;}
```

Note that the first line box is made tall enough to contain the image, whereas the second is tall enough to contain the image, its padding, and its border.

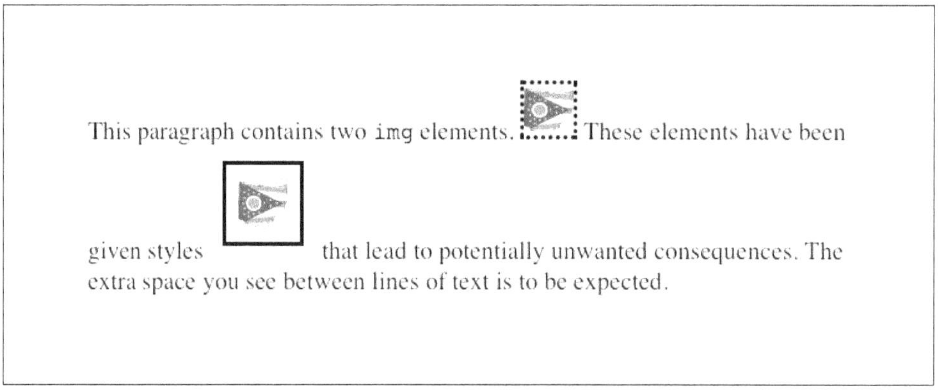

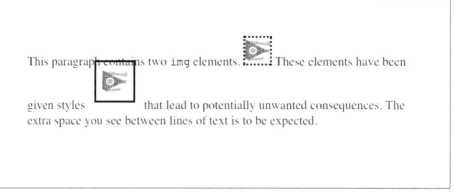

Figure 52. Adding padding, borders, and margins to an inline replaced element increases its inline box

Margins are also contained within the line box, but they have their own wrinkles. Setting a positive margin is no mystery; it will simply make the inline box of the replaced element taller. Setting negative margins, meanwhile, has a similar effect: it decreases the size of the replaced element's inline box. This is illustrated in Figure 53, where we can see that a negative top margin is pulling down the line above the image:

```
img.two {margin-top: -10px;}
```

Negative margins operate the same way on block-level elements, of course. In this case, the negative margins make the replaced element's inline box smaller than ordinary. Negative margins are the only way to cause inline replaced elements to bleed into other lines, and it's why the boxes that replaced inline elements generate are often assumed to be inline-block.

Figure 53. The effect of negative margins on inline replaced elements

Replaced Elements and the Baseline

You may have noticed by now that, by default, inline replaced elements sit on the baseline. If you add bottom padding, a margin, or a border to the replaced element, then the content area will move upward (assuming box-sizing: content-box). Replaced elements do not actually have baselines of their own, so the next best thing is to align the bottom of their inline boxes with the baseline. Thus, it is actually the bottom outer margin edge that is aligned with the baseline, as illustrated in Figure 54.

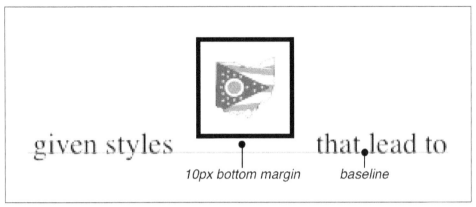

Figure 54. Inline replaced elements sit on the baseline

This baseline alignment leads to an unexpected (and unwelcome) consequence: an image placed in a table cell all by itself should make the table cell tall enough to contain the line box containing the image. The resizing occurs even if there is no actual text, not even whitespace, in the table cell with the image. Therefore, the common sliced-image and spacer-GIF designs of years past can fall apart quite dramatically in modern browsers. (I know that *you* don't create such things, but this is still a handy context in which to explain this behavior.) Consider the simplest case:

```
td {font-size: 12px;}
```

```
<td><img src="spacer.gif" height="1" width="10"></td>
```

Under the CSS inline formatting model, the table cell will be 12 pixels tall, with the image sitting on the baseline of the cell. So there might be three pixels of space below the image and eight above it, although the exact distances would depend on the font family used and the placement of its baseline.

This behavior is not confined to images inside table cells; it will also happen in any situation where an inline replaced element is the sole descendant of a block-level or table-cell element. For example, an image inside a div will also sit on the baseline.

The most common workaround for such circumstances is simply to make images in table cells block-level so that they do not generate a line box. For example:

```
td {font-size: 12px;}
img.block {display: block;}

<td><img src="spacer.gif" height="1" width="10" class="block"></td>
```

Another possible fix would be to make the font-size and line-height of the enclosing table cell 1px, which would make the line box only as tall as the one-pixel image within it.

 As of this writing, many browsers can ignore this CSS inline formatting model in this context. See the article "Images, Tables, and Mysterious Gaps" (*http://bit.ly/imgs-tables-gaps*) for more information.

Here's another interesting effect of inline replaced elements sitting on the baseline: if we apply a negative bottom margin, the element will actually get pulled downward because the bottom of its inline box will be higher than the bottom of its content area. Thus, the following rule would have the result shown in Figure 55:

```
p img {margin-bottom: -10px;}
```

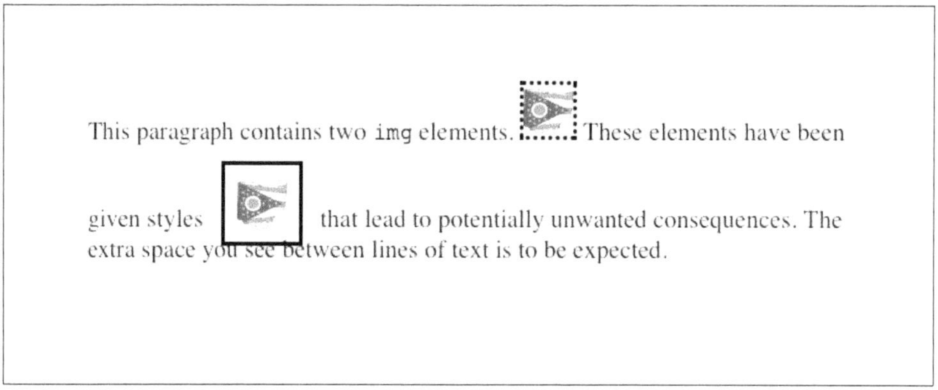

This paragraph contains two img elements. These elements have been given styles that lead to potentially unwanted consequences. The extra space you see between lines of text is to be expected.

Figure 55. Pulling inline replaced elements down with a negative bottom margin

This can easily cause a replaced element to bleed into following lines of text, as Figure 55 shows.

Inline with History

The CSS inline formatting model may seem needlessly complex and, in some ways, even contrary to author expectations. Unfortunately, the complexity is the result of creating a style language that is both backward-compatible with pre-CSS web browsers and leaves the door open for future expansion into more sophisticated territory—an awkward blend of past and present. It's also the result of making some sensible decisions that avoid one undesirable effect while causing another.

For example, the "spreading apart" of lines of text by image and vertically aligned text owes its roots to the way Mosaic 1.0 behaved. In that browser, any image in a paragraph would simply push open enough space to contain the image. That's a good behavior, since it prevents images from overlapping text in other lines. So when CSS introduced ways to style text and inline elements, its authors endeavored to create a model that did not (by default) cause inline images to overlap other lines of text. However, the same model also meant that a superscript element (sup), for example, would likely also push apart lines of text.

Such effects annoy some authors who want their baselines to be an exact distance apart and no further, but consider the alternative. If line-height forced baselines to be exactly a specified distance apart, we'd easily end up with inline replaced and vertically shifted elements that overlap other lines of text—which would also annoy authors. Fortunately, CSS offers enough power to create your desired effect in one way or another, and the future of CSS holds even more potential.

Inline-Block Elements

As befits the hybrid look of the value name inline-block, inline-block elements are indeed a hybrid of block-level and inline elements. This display value was introduced in CSS2.1.

An inline-block element relates to other elements and content as an inline box. In other words, it's laid out in a line of text just as an image would be, and in fact, inline-block elements are formatted within a line as a replaced element. This means the bottom of the inline-block element will rest on the baseline of the text line by default and will not linebreak within itself.

Inside the inline-block element, the content is formatted as though the element were block-level. The properties width and height apply to it (and thus so does box-sizing), as they do to any block-level or inline replaced element, and those properties will increase the height of the line if they are taller than the surrounding content.

Let's consider some example markup that will help make this clearer:

```
<div id="one">
This text is the content of a block-level level element. Within this
block-level element is another block-level element. <p>Look, it's a block-level
paragraph.</p> Here's the rest of the DIV, which is still block-level.
</div>
<div id="two">
This text is the content of a block-level level element. Within this
block-level element is an inline element. <p>Look, it's an inline
paragraph.</p> Here's the rest of the DIV, which is still block-level.
</div>
<div id="three">
This text is the content of a block-level level element. Within this
block-level element is an inline-block element. <p>Look, it's an inline-block
paragraph.</p> Here's the rest of the DIV, which is still block-level.
</div>
```

To this markup, we apply the following rules:

```
div {margin: 1em 0; border: 1px solid;}
p {border: 1px dotted;}
div#one p {display: block; width: 6em; text-align: center;}
div#two p {display: inline; width: 6em; text-align: center;}
div#three p {display: inline-block; width: 6em; text-align: center;}
```

The result of this stylesheet is depicted in Figure 56.

Notice that in the second `div`, the inline paragraph is formatted as normal inline content, which means `width` and `text-align` get ignored (since they do not apply to inline elements). For the third `div`, however, the inline-block paragraph honors both properties, since it is formatted as a block-level element. That paragraph's margins also force its line of text to be much taller, since it affects line height as though it were a replaced element.

If an inline-block element's `width` is not defined or explicitly declared `auto`, the element box will shrink to fit the content. That is, the element box is exactly as wide as necessary to hold the content, and no wider. Inline boxes act the same way, although they can break across lines of text, whereas inline-block elements cannot. Thus, we have the following rule, when applied to the previous markup example:

```
div#three p {display: inline-block; height: 4em;}
```

will create a tall box that's just wide enough to enclose the content, as shown in Figure 57.

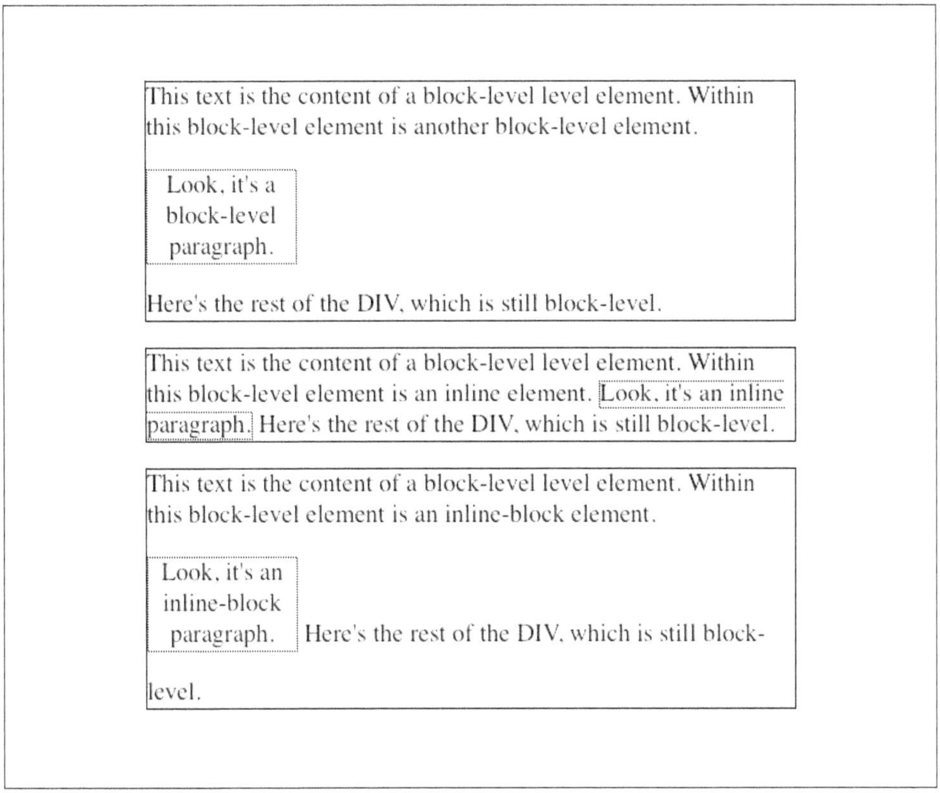

This text is the content of a block-level level element. Within this block-level element is another block-level element.

Look, it's a block-level paragraph.

Here's the rest of the DIV, which is still block-level.

This text is the content of a block-level level element. Within this block-level element is an inline element. Look, it's an inline paragraph. Here's the rest of the DIV, which is still block-level.

This text is the content of a block-level level element. Within this block-level element is an inline-block element.

Look, it's an inline-block paragraph. Here's the rest of the DIV, which is still block-level.

Figure 56. The behavior of an inline-block element

Inline-block elements can be useful if, for example, we have a set of five hyperlinks that we want to be equal width within a toolbar. To make them all 20% the width of their parent element, but still leave them inline, declare:

```
nav a {display: inline-block; width: 20%;}
```

 Flexible-box layout is another way to achieve this effect, and is probably better suited to it in most if not all cases.

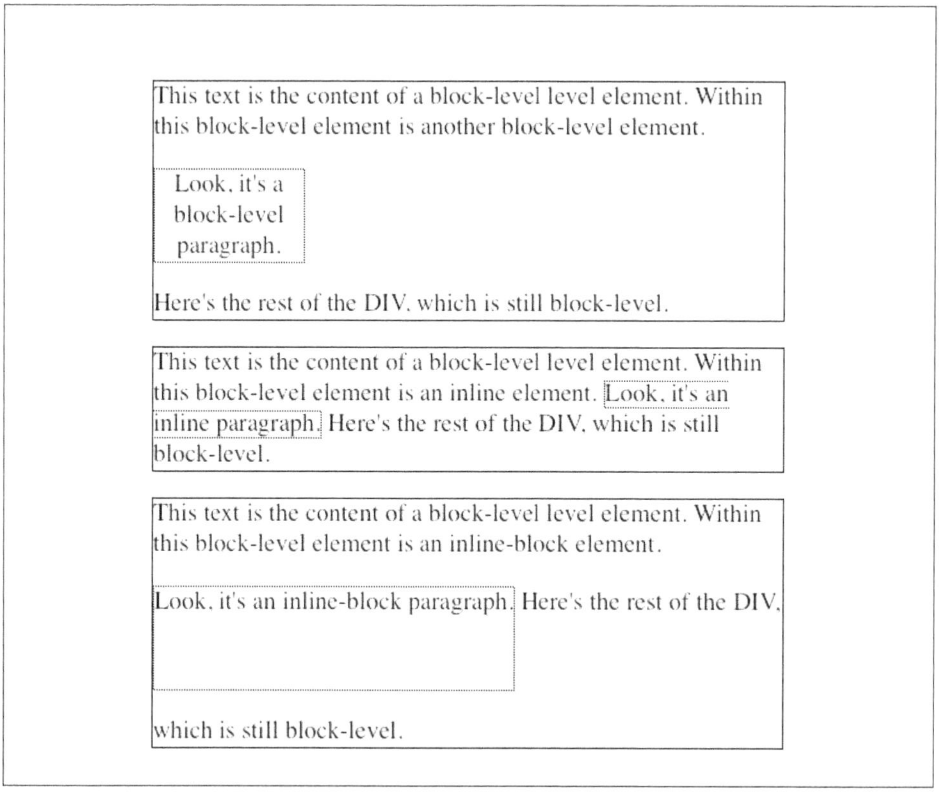

Figure 57. Autosizing of an inline-block element

Run-in Elements

CSS2 introduced the value `run-in`, another interesting block/inline hybrid that can make some block-level elements an inline part of a following element. This ability is useful for certain heading effects that are quite common in print typography, where a heading will appear as part of a paragraph of text.

In CSS, you can make an element run-in simply by changing its `display` value *and* by making the next element box block-level. Note that I'm talking about *boxes* here, not the elements themselves. In other words, it doesn't matter if an element is block or inline. All that matters is the box that element generates. A `strong` element set to `display: block` generates a block-level box; a paragraph set to `display: inline` generates an inline box.

So, to rephrase this: if an element generates a run-in box, and a block box follows that box, then the run-in element will be an inline box at the beginning of the block box. For example:

```
<h3 style="display: run-in; border: 1px dotted; font-size: 125%;
font-weight: bold;">Run-in Elements</h3>
<p style="border-top: 1px solid black; padding-top: 0.5em;">
Another interesting block/inline hybrid is the value <code>run-in</code>,
introduced in CSS2, which has the ability to take block-level elements and make
them an inline part of a following element. This is useful for certain heading
effects that are quite common in print typography, where a heading will appear
as part of a paragraph of text.
</p>
```

Since the p element following the h3 generates a block-level box, the h3 element will be turned into an inline element at the beginning of the p element's content, as illustrated in Figure 58.

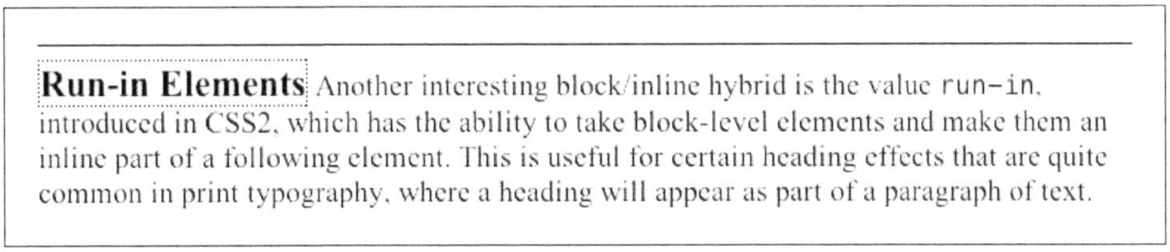

Figure 58. Making a heading run-in

Note how the borders of the two elements are placed. The effect of using run-in in this situation is exactly the same as if we'd used this markup instead:

```
<p style="border-top: 1px solid black; padding-top: 0.5em;">
<span style="border: 1px dotted; font-size: 125%; font-weight: bold;">Run-in
Elements</span> Another interesting block/inline hybrid is the value
<code>run-in</code>, introduced in CSS2, which has the ability to take block-
level elements and make them an inline part of a following element. This is
useful for certain heading effects that are quite common in print typography,
where a heading will appear as part of a paragraph of text.
</p>
```

However, there is a slight difference between run-in boxes and the markup example. Even though run-in boxes are formatted as inline boxes within another element, they still inherit properties from their parent element in the document, not the element into which they're placed. Let's extend our example to include an enclosing div and some color:

```
<div style="color: silver;">
<h3 style="display: run-in; border: 1px dotted; font-size: 125%;
font-weight: bold;">Run-in Elements</h3>
<p style="border-top: 1px solid black; padding-top: 0.5em; color: black;">
Another interesting block/inline hybrid is the value <code>run-in</code>,
introduced in CSS2, which has the ability to take block-level elements and make
them an inline part of a following element.
</p>
</div>
```

In this situation, the h3 will be silver, not black, as illustrated in Figure 59. That's because it inherits the color value from its parent element before it gets inserted into the paragraph.

Another interesting block/inline hybrid is the value run-in, introduced in CSS2, which has the ability to take block-level elements and make them an inline part of a following element.

Figure 59. Run-in elements inherit from their source parents

The important thing to remember is that run-in will work only if the box after the run-in box is block-level. If it is not, then the run-in box itself will be made block-level. Thus, given the following markup, the h3 will remain or even become block-level, since the display value for the table element is (oddly enough) table:

```
<h3 style="display: run-in;">Prices</h3>
<table>
<tr><th>Apples</th><td>$0.59</td></tr>
<tr><th>Peaches</th><td>$0.79</td></tr>
<tr><th>Pumpkin</th><td>$1.29</td></tr>
<tr><th>Pie</th><td>$6.99</td></tr>
</table>
```

It's unlikely that an author would ever apply the value run-in to a naturally inline element, but if this happens, the element will most likely generate a block-level box. For example, the em element in the following markup would become block-level because a block-level box does not follow it:

```
<p>
This is a <em>really</em> odd thing to do, <strong>but</strong> you could do it
if you were so inclined.
</p>
```

 At the time of this writing, very few browsers offer support for run-in.

Computed Values

The computed value of display can change if an element is floated or positioned. It can also change when declared for the root element. In fact, the values display, position, and float interact in interesting ways.

If an element is absolutely positioned, the value of float is set to none. For either floated or absolutely positioned elements, the computed value of display is determined by the declared value, as shown in Table 1.

Table 1. Computed display values for floated or positioned elements

Declared value	Computed value
inline-table	table
inline, run-in, table-row-group, table-column, table-column-group, table-header-group, table-footer-group, table-row, table-cell, table-caption, inline-block	block
All others	As specified

In the case of the root element, declaring either of the values inline-table or table results in a computed value of table, whereas declaring none results in the same computed value. All other display values are computed to be block.

Summary

Although some aspects of the CSS formatting model may seem counterintuitive at first, they begin to make sense the more one works with them. In many cases, rules that seem nonsensical or even idiotic turn out to exist in order to prevent bizarre or otherwise undesirable document displays. Block-level elements are in many ways easy to understand, and affecting their layout is typically a simple task. Inline elements, on the other hand, can be trickier to manage, as a number of factors come into play, not least of which is whether the element is replaced or nonreplaced.

About the Author

Eric A. Meyer has been working with the Web since late 1993 and is an internationally recognized expert on the subjects of HTML, CSS, and web standards. A widely read author, he is also the founder of Complex Spiral Consulting (*http://www.complex spiral.com*), which counts among its clients America Online; Apple Computer, Inc.; Wells Fargo Bank; and Macromedia, which described Eric as "a critical partner in our efforts to transform Macromedia Dreamweaver MX 2004 into a revolutionary tool for CSS-based design."

Beginning in early 1994, Eric was the visual designer and campus web coordinator for the Case Western Reserve University website, where he also authored a widely acclaimed series of three HTML tutorials and was project coordinator for the online version of the *Encyclopedia of Cleveland History* and the *Dictionary of Cleveland Biography*, the first encyclopedia of urban history published fully and freely on the Web.

Author of *Eric Meyer on CSS* and *More Eric Meyer on CSS* (New Riders), *CSS: The Definitive Guide* (*http://bit.ly/css-tdg-3e*) (O'Reilly), and *CSS2.0 Programmer's Reference* (Osborne/McGraw-Hill), as well as numerous articles for the O'Reilly Network, Web Techniques, and Web Review, Eric also created the CSS Browser Compatibility Charts and coordinated the authoring and creation of the W3C's official CSS Test Suite. He has lectured to a wide variety of organizations, including Los Alamos National Laboratory, the New York Public Library, Cornell University, and the University of Northern Iowa. Eric has also delivered addresses and technical presentations at numerous conferences, among them An Event Apart (which he cofounded), the IW3C2 WWW series, Web Design World, CMP, SXSW, the User Interface conference series, and The Other Dreamweaver Conference.

In his personal time, Eric acts as list chaperone of the highly active css-discuss mailing list (*http://www.css-discuss.org*), which he cofounded with John Allsopp of Western Civilisation, and which is now supported by *evolt.org*. Eric lives in Cleveland, Ohio, which is a much nicer city than you've been led to believe. For nine years he was the host of "Your Father's Oldsmobile," a big-band radio show heard weekly on WRUW 91.1 FM in Cleveland.

You can find more detailed information on Eric's personal web page (*http://www.meyerweb.com/eric*).

Colophon

The animals on the cover of *Basic Visual Formatting in CSS* are salmon (*salmonidae*), which is a family of fish consisting of many different species. Two of the most common salmon are the Pacific salmon and the Atlantic salmon.

Pacific salmon live in the northern Pacific Ocean off the coasts of North America and Asia. There are five subspecies of Pacific salmon, with an average weight of 10 to 30 pounds. Pacific salmon are born in the fall in freshwater stream gravel beds, where they incubate through the winter and emerge as inch-long fish. They live for a year or two in streams or lakes and then head downstream to the ocean. There they live for a few years, before heading back upstream to their exact place of birth to spawn and then die.

Atlantic salmon live in the northern Atlantic Ocean off the coasts of North America and Europe. There are many subspecies of Atlantic salmon, including the trout and the char. Their average weight is 10 to 20 pounds. The Atlantic salmon family has a life cycle similar to that of its Pacific cousins, and also travels from freshwater gravel beds to the sea. A major difference between the two, however, is that the Atlantic salmon does not die after spawning; it can return to the ocean and then return to the stream to spawn again, usually two or three times.

Salmon, in general, are graceful, silver-colored fish with spots on their backs and fins. Their diet consists of plankton, insect larvae, shrimp, and smaller fish. Their unusually keen sense of smell is thought to help them navigate from the ocean back to the exact spot of their birth, upstream past many obstacles. Some species of salmon remain landlocked, living their entire lives in freshwater.

Salmon are an important part of the ecosystem, as their decaying bodies provide fertilizer for streambeds. Their numbers have been dwindling over the years, however. Factors in the declining salmon population include habitat destruction, fishing, dams that block spawning paths, acid rain, droughts, floods, and pollution.

The cover image is a 19th-century engraving from the Dover Pictorial Archive. The cover fonts are URW Typewriter and Guardian Sans. The text font is Adobe Minion Pro; the heading font is Adobe Myriad Condensed; and the code font is Dalton Maag's Ubuntu Mono.

Have it your way.

Get even more for your money.

Join the O'Reilly Community, and register the O'Reilly books you own. It's free, and you'll get:

- $4.99 ebook upgrade offer
- 40% upgrade offer on O'Reilly print books
- Membership discounts on books and events
- Free lifetime updates to ebooks and videos
- Multiple ebook formats, DRM FREE
- Participation in the O'Reilly community
- Newsletters
- Account management
- 100% Satisfaction Guarantee

Signing up is easy:

1. Go to: oreilly.com/go/register
2. Create an O'Reilly login.
3. Provide your address.
4. Register your books.

Note: English-language books only

To order books online:
oreilly.com/store

For questions about products or an order:
orders@oreilly.com

To sign up to get topic-specific email announcements and/or news about upcoming books, conferences, special offers, and new technologies:
elists@oreilly.com

For technical questions about book content:
booktech@oreilly.com

To submit new book proposals to our editors:
proposals@oreilly.com

O'Reilly books are available in multiple DRM-free ebook formats. For more information:
oreilly.com/ebooks

Milton Keynes UK
Ingram Content Group UK Ltd.
UKHW030638051024
449225UK00007B/134